FIRE + WINE

BACKYARD PIZZA

FIRE + WINE

BACKYARD PIZZA

Perfect Pizza for Any Outdoor Oven or Grill,
with Inspired Wine Pairings

MARY CRESSLER and **SEAN MARTIN**

SASQUATCH BOOKS
SEATTLE

CONTENTS

DELIGHTFUL DOUGHS AND SAUCES

FLAT-OUT FANTASTIC
Elevated Flatbreads, Starters, and Sides

KEEPING IT CLASSY
Classic Pizzas Everyone Should Know

A SAVORY SYMPHONY
Harmonizing Flavors

A VEGGIE VOYAGE

PUT AN EGG ON IT
Breakfast Pizzas That Impress

SUGAR RUSH
Dessert Pizzas

INTRODUCTION

Years ago we were introduced to the artful joy of the outdoor pizza party when our good friends invested in a giant pizza oven. When we say *giant,* we mean it was so big that when it arrived in their front yard, they needed to rent a crane (a CRANE!) to transfer it up and over their house into their backyard!

Now that would have become a viral #story for Instagram; if only stories had existed back then! And by *back then,* we don't mean the 1980s or '90s. This was circa *2014.*

At that time, in order for you to have a quality pizza oven in your backyard you would have had to build it yourself or buy one for thousands of dollars. In our friends' case, they spent just under $5,000 total.

That's a huge investment for the average family. Just for pizzas.

Flash forward a decade and manufacturers have now designed pizza ovens and grill attachments that rival those of the best restaurants in the world, for fractions of the cost (not to mention fractions of the size as well). Many of them are even portable. You can take them camping, to the beach, or just to your neighbors' houses (much to their delight).

They come in a variety of shapes and sizes, and most of the commercial market ovens perform pretty darn well for making restaurant-quality pizzas in the comfort of your own backyard. Every year legacy manufacturers, like Weber and Big Green Egg, design more pizza attachments that grow in quality and popularity for grills, giving anyone the opportunity to feed their inner pizza chef.

We are so lucky to be living in a time when you no longer need to rent a crane to deliver a quality pizza oven to your backyard; although, we're grateful for our passionate friends who made that investment. We learned a lot from them, and it was the catalyst for igniting our own pizza flame.

And, for the same price as a beginner grill, you too can be making restaurant-quality pizzas in your backyard in no time.

What that time with our friends taught us—besides a lesson in making sure a giant pizza oven would fit through your side gate—was that pizza parties are a pretty magical way to bring friends, family, and neighbors together. Dare we say even better than throwing a traditional backyard BBQ?!

Because everyone likes pizza. Hard stop.

You see, in those days, if you were going to fire up that pizza oven, which, for their particular giant oven, took a full hour to come to temperature, you'd better invite a lot of people because you're going to be baking lots of pizzas to make up for the time spent warming the darn thing up.

So pizza parties they had.

It was an art.

It became a neighborhood event. They made the dough and sauce, and for everyone else it was BYOT (bring your own toppings). Going to those parties just to see some of the combinations people invented was worth the time. People would get *very* creative. Some were winners. Few were busts.

But, hey, it was pizza! Even the busts were still worth eating.

When we started making pizzas in our own backyard, we began by baking them on our grill. It was all we had to experiment with at the time. Since then we've made pizzas on our Big Green Egg, our Weber kettle grill, gas grill, and even pellet grills. We know, we have a lot of grills. The pizzas all came out pretty darn decent, if we do say so ourselves.

We've learned techniques along the way, including what temperatures work best on each cooker, and have tested different types of dough to match each grill style.

Flash forward to today, we now have the full range of pizza cookers, from dedicated pizza ovens that get up to 900 degrees F (such as the Gozney Dome, Ooni Karu, and Solo Stove Pi, among others), providing the perfect environment for Neapolitan-inspired pies, to our line of backyard grills, which max out around 600 degrees F but can still push out some delicious pies in the New York, Chicago, and even Detroit styles.

Our goal with this book is to meet you where you are. If you have a simple kettle grill or a dedicated pizza oven, this book is for you. We will go through the fundamentals of making great pizza outside, walk through our tried-and-true doughs and sauces, and offer enough recipes to get you started on your own pizza journey. If it piques your interest, we have loads of additional tutorials on our website Vindulge.com, and if you want to geek out deeper on doughs and the history of pizza, we can introduce you to some of the best teachers and resources out there.

We don't need to reinvent the wheel as there are some fantastic cooks who've already gone there. We want to build on their incredible work, and show you how to get started today in your backyard, with whatever cooker you have.

So whether you have a dedicated outdoor pizza oven or any number of grills, we have created recipes that will work on all of them. Bonus: we even discuss how to adapt the pizzas for your kitchen oven.

You can learn to make great pizzas at home. And they will be delicious!

Welcome to *Fire + Wine Backyard Pizza*.

MARY AND SEAN

Styles of Pizza for This Book

To make a book about all the styles of pizza would be more akin to writing a series of encyclopedias versus an easy-to-navigate book for the outdoor enthusiast. There are so many styles of pizza, from the classic Neapolitan to New York, Chicago deep dish, Detroit, Sicilian, you name it . . . There are dozens of styles.

Mary has had the incredible opportunity to travel the world learning about pizza from some of the best regions. Her first time dining in Naples was magical to say the least. Then to Sicily, where she still—to this day—dreams about the food there. Living in Connecticut allowed us both the opportunity to eat at the renowned Frank Pepe's, as well as dozens of trips to New York to try some of the tastiest pies. Mary was also born and raised in Phoenix, Arizona, so a visit to see the family usually involves a trip to Pizzeria Bianco, one of the most famous West Coast pizza joints. And we would argue that a handful of pizzerias in Portland, Oregon, where we now call home, can rival some of the best in the world.

When it comes to our BBQ and what we are known for, our style is not the same as those in Texas, the Carolinas, or even Kansas City. We do Pacific Northwest (PNW) BBQ. And that applies to pizza as well. Pizza is not classically a BBQ category, but it has become an outdoor staple over the past few years with the rise in popularity of pizza ovens. The biggest grill manufacturers have jumped on the pizza bandwagon, producing accessories for various styles of grills, making it easier to create restaurant-quality pizza on a backyard grill.

So while we've had the privilege of experiencing and enjoying pizza in some of the best regions of the world, we don't claim to be experts in all styles of pizza. Rather, our goal is to honor those styles that have inspired us and combine that love with our decades of experience cooking on grills, smokers, and dedicated outdoor pizza ovens, in the hope that it becomes an inspiration to you.

How to Use This Book

Whether you are just getting started on your pizza-making journey or you've been doing it for years, we encourage you to begin with the Fire chapter (page 11). It contains the fundamentals of baking pizza on any outdoor grill or pizza oven. Successful pizza making is about understanding the heat levels that your grill or cooker can manage, and having just the right tools to accomplish this (spoiler alert: you don't need that many). It's also understanding the best kinds of doughs needed for outdoor pizza making based on how hot your fire can get. From there, it's experimenting with your favorite styles of pizzas.

We have written this book so that you can make amazing pizzas on almost any outdoor grill or pizza oven. You won't need a specific brand or type of cooker. New products and tools are introduced all the time that make the process a little easier, but the fundamentals don't change. You simply need to understand the thermal dynamics that your cooker can handle to match the style of pizza you wish to make.

Our goal is to give you the tools to manage your heat source and be able to prepare homemade dough that will cook perfectly. From there, you can customize your sauce and toppings to become a pizza hero in your own backyard.

After that, you can choose to Vindulge in the Wine chapter (page 39), where we go through the fundamentals of delicious wine pairing and how they apply to pizza. Then it's on to the fun part.

We've included more than forty recipes to get you started on your pizza journey. The most important thing, though, is to make sure you are having fun and always learning and experimenting. So grab yourself a glass of wine or your favorite beverage, discover your preferred type of grill or pizza oven, and begin planning your first or seventeenth pizza party. Get people involved, teach them how to shape the dough, and sling a pie. Not only will this up your pizza game, but it will make you a pizza god among your family and friends.

FIRE

THERE IS NO BETTER FEELING than making pizza outdoors on a warm and sunny day. For us, it's always with a group of friends and family. It's the ability to engage with each other, to share secrets on how to shape the dough, or find out what toppings people love or those they can't stand. It's never having to deal with a picky eater, because everyone likes pizza. It's breaking bread and drinking some great wines while watching our kids run around and sneak an extra slice when we aren't looking. It's the experience of communal feeling that has been around for centuries.

Most cookbooks about grilled pizza focus on one technique—parbaking your dough over the grill grates, then adding your toppings and finishing it back on the grill grates. That works great if all you have is a grill and grates. But throw in a pizza stone and suddenly you have an outdoor pizza oven.

And with the growth of companies such as Ooni, Gozney, and Solo Stove, along with the development of pizza modifications for traditional grills, there has never been a more affordable time to own a dedicated pizza cooker that can produce restaurant-quality pies, right in your backyard.

No matter what type of grill or pizza oven you have, the key elements that make (or burn) a great pizza are going to be the heat and the right dough. Oh, and don't add too many ingredients to your pizza. Seriously, don't. But we'll get to that later.

Heat

Making the perfect outdoor pizza requires lots of consistent heat. Some styles of pizzas, like Neapolitan, need incredible levels of heat that some grills just can't attain. The most important technique to master is managing your heat source based on the style of your grill or pizza oven and its fuel source. From there, it's about picking the right dough to match your level of heat.

A stand-alone pizza oven is built to achieve internal temperatures of 1,000 degrees F (537 degrees C), or higher. But attempt that same temperature in a Big Green Egg and you will damage it, especially if done repeatedly. So let's discuss the most common types of fuel before we introduce the grills and pizza ovens out there.

CHARCOAL. Charcoal comes in lump or uniform-sized briquettes or bars. Charcoal is the most common fuel source for kettle grills and *kamado*-style grills, like the Big Green Egg. Because of how these grills are designed, it's uncommon and not recommended for the internal temperature of those grills to exceed 650 degrees F (343 degrees C). The large chunks and natural wood flavor of lump charcoal is more prominent compared to briquettes, which are great for more consistent heat but lack some of the flavor. We use lump charcoal and recommend that you do too. And don't use lighter fluid to start up your charcoal. More on that later.

- **PROS:** Adds great flavor to your pizzas when using lump charcoal. Lights and gets hot quickly.
- **CONS:** Once lit, charcoal can burn fast and will get really hot with your lid frequently open or vents fully open. Charcoal takes a little more babysitting to reach the ideal cooking temperature for pizza.

PELLETS. Pellets are made from ground wood that has been pressed into pellets to fuel pellet grills or pizza ovens. When you add a heat source like a match or a hot rod, you have the ability to produce wood-fired smoke. This is how pellet grills work, and many pizza ovens are made and adapted to fuel with wood pellets. Pellets are ideal for lower-heat New York–style pizza doughs. Pellet grills do not reach 1,000 degrees F, and if using pellets in a pizza oven, it requires an incredible amount of pellets to get embers to burn that hot.

- **PROS:** Cheap fuel source that is easy to feed into pizza ovens (and for pellet grills, the only way to run the heat source). Consistent temperatures that can maintain 450–500 degrees F depending on the pellet grill and quality of the pellets.
- **CONS:** They don't burn as fast or hot as traditional pizza ovens. If using a pizza oven, it's best to work with wood chunks designed for the size of your unit versus pellets. If pellets get wet, they will be ruined.

WOOD SPLITS. In many dedicated pizza ovens, you can use wood cut at specific sizes optimized for the size of your pizza oven. When using wood, you get a hot fire from the embers and a nice flame as you ignite a new piece of wood to add to the convection cooking needed for both the crust and top of the pizza.

- **PROS:** More efficient than wood pellets and easy-to-maintain hot embers and flame compared with charcoal.
- **CONS:** It requires more labor to cook and maintain the fire and

embers while you are also trying to make pizzas. This scenario works best if you have two people, one for managing the fire while turning pizzas, and the other for building the actual pizzas.

PROPANE. Propane (or natural gas) can burn hot and be an efficient source of heat commonly seen on gas grills and dual-fuel pizza ovens. Propane is convenient because it burns consistently and doesn't require as much labor as tending a wood fire. Propane is also becoming available for pellet grills running a gas pizza-oven attachment, like the Camp Chef brand.

- **PROS:** An efficient and affordable heat source. Stable temperatures throughout the cooking process. Very little babysitting or heat management needed.
- **CONS:** Wind can easily blow out the flame in pizza ovens, and for poorly designed gas pizza ovens the flame can grow too big or too small.

No matter what type of pizza oven or grill you are using, it is important to understand these essential heat sources and be aware of their pros and cons.

How to Light Your Fire

Unless your grill or pizza oven has an internal starter (like most gas grills or propane pizza ovens), you need to manually ignite the fire. This can be done a few ways, and none of them involve lighter fluid.

Lighter fluid uses chemicals to cause combustion after the charcoal is lit. That chemical smell and flavor will permeate the pizza stone or ceramic, depending on your style of grill. It doesn't take that much longer to start a fire using alternatives to lighter fluid, like a chimney starter or tumbleweeds.

LIGHTING CHARCOAL. Charcoal is best for any traditional charcoal grill. You can use a charcoal chimney to light the charcoal quickly and place it in your grill. You then feed more charcoal (if needed) and let the grill reach your desired temperature.

1   Place a small amount of paper in the shallow side of the chimney starter, then add your lump charcoal in the larger side.

2   Place the chimney with charcoal side up inside your grill or on a fire-safe surface, like concrete, and light the paper. The fire will be concentrated into the charcoal lighting it.

3   The charcoal is ready when it's all lit and the coals have turned white. Dump the charcoal into your grill based on the recommended setup.

4   If you plan to make many pizzas and need the temperature of the grill to maintain 500 degrees F for more than an hour, follow the same starting process and drop the lit charcoal into your grill. Then add fresh, unlit charcoal over the top, and set it up based on your cooking method. Add more charcoal as needed to maintain the fire. Anytime you add unlit charcoal, the temperature will go down. So be sure to mix up the lit and unlit charcoal using a metal rod or ash tool.

CHEF'S TIP: Make sure when using lump charcoal that you have a mix of large and small chunks in the chimney. The smaller pieces should be on the bottom near the paper. If all you have are large chunks, the fire will not start because there are not enough smaller pieces in the void to create the necessary intense heat.

It's also a good idea to have a pair of welding-style gloves specifically made for grilling at high heat. These gloves can often handle temperatures over 900 degrees F and are helpful if you need to lift up a grill grate or pizza stone to add more charcoal.

Alternatively, you can use tumbleweed fire starters as we do with wood. Just put one or two of them in the charcoal and light them. Carefully place a few larger pieces of charcoal over the top so the starter can burn and ignite the surrounding charcoal. After 30–40 minutes, the grill should be hot enough for pizza.

WOOD. Wood is best for dedicated pizza ovens. The easiest way to start your fire is to use a tumbleweed fire starter. Set up the wood in a log cabin three rows high. Nestle the tumbleweed inside the "cabin." Light the tumbleweed and allow the initial wood to ignite. As it burns, it will collapse into a nice pile of embers. Continue to add more wood to heat your pizza oven or grill to your desired temperature.

Eventually, you will move that wood to one side of your oven. This keeps an open area for your pizzas to cook and creates forced convection around the oven.

The downside to wood is that you need to continually add it to the fire every 10 minutes, which means more human resources. Upside: you get a much more even cooking experience on the crust from the embers.

PROPANE VERSUS WOOD. Is there a difference in flavor? We get asked this question all the time. And the simple (controversial answer) is no.

Most commonly, you are burning wood for a Neapolitan-style pizza, which cooks in 2 minutes or less. In that time you get very little wood-smoke flavor. What you do get is a more even cooking along the crust from a well-built base of embers tucked along the side or back of your oven. So if there is any flavor difference, it's really in the texture of the crust.

Before you run and grab the right fuel, the other key tool you need besides your grill or pizza oven is a good pizza stone. Dedicated pizza ovens already have the stone built into the unit, called the deck. But for grills, you need to buy your own. We discuss pizza stones and steels, and what to look for when purchasing one, in the Tools and Ingredients chapter (page 59).

Managing Heat

Now that you have selected your fuel source and started your fire, you need to maintain the right heat level based on your style of grill or oven. This equates to heating your pizza stone or deck to the best temperature for your pizza. It's also important to know what heat levels your grill or oven can reach. If you get a grill too hot, you can break a stone—or worse, crack or warp your grill. This is why we don't recommend allowing a Big Green Egg, for example, to exceed 600 degrees F, and the reason you can't make a traditional Neapolitan-style pizza on a kamado or kettle grill.

The secondary reason to maintain the right level of heat based on your grill or pizza oven is to make sure you cook the crust through *as well as* the toppings. If your unit is too hot, you can burn the crust before the toppings have cooked and the cheese has melted. If the temperature is too cool, the pizza texture will become unpleasant and you run the risk of burning the toppings before the crust is done. So it's important to balance the right temperature with the right dough with the right amount of cooking time.

CONVECTION HEAT

Convection is the process of heat moving from one place to another. In the case of cooking, it's heated air and cooler air that move around the cooking chamber either by fans or the design of the cooking chamber.

When making pizzas on a grill or pizza oven, the convection process is what helps to cook the bottom and the top of your pizza evenly. Heated air moves around the unit, keeping the pizza stone hot while also cooking the top of the pizza. Some grills are better designed than others when it comes to how air circulates in the cooking chamber.

The pizza stone (or pizza steel on a kettle grill) maintains the heat level needed to cook the bottom and sides of the pizza. The heat over the top caused by convection and the flame is what cooks the top of the pizza. The goal is to balance both so you have an evenly cooked pizza.

CHEF'S TIP: Pizza stones maintain heat well, but it takes time for the entire stone to radiate that heat. If you start throwing pizzas onto the stone right when it hits your target temperature, expect the stone to cool down by 100 degrees F (or more). You need to pause and let the stone return to the desired temperature. The longer the stone is under heat, the more radiant heat in the stone will maintain the temperature and the faster you can cook your next pizza. Always take the temperature of your stone or deck before placing another pizza.

That's why the first pizza we cook is always either a test pizza or the kids' pizza (sorry, kids), because the stone may still be cool in some places and you may see some uneven cooking. We test it out with that first pizza to gauge where we are in the process. Ideally, let your stone maintain the right temperature for 30–45 minutes if you are planning to make multiple pizzas for a party.

MANAGING CHARCOAL AND WOOD AIRFLOW

With the exception of propane, the general rule of live-fire heat is the more airflow that enters the heat source, the hotter your grill or oven becomes. So if you have venting on your grill, start a grill with the vents wide open. Follow the lighting process. Then, as the fire starts and the fuel source ignites, adjust your grill setup so the pizza stone (or steel) can warm up with the grill.

As the temperature begins to rise in the grill and your pizza stone hits your temperature target, partially close the vents to maintain just enough air to hold that temperature. You can open and close them as you need to, but know that it's easier to add more airflow and warm up your grill than it is to try and cool a grill that overshoots the heat mark.

We always start with all vents wide open and then, after the initial burn, slowly close them until we hit the right temperature of the stone. The vents will be open or closed more based on wind and weather.

USING PELLETS IN A PELLET GRILL

Pellets provide a consistent source of heat, especially in pellet grills or pellet smokers. All you need to do is make sure your pellet hopper (the chamber where the pellets sit) is full and that your ash is cleaned out of the burn pot (where the wood pellets drop to ignite). Get in the habit of cleaning out that burn pot before every grilling to avoid ash covering the igniter rod.

Follow the startup sequence recommended by the manufacturer, then turn up the heat to the highest it will go. Make sure your pizza stone is in the grill as it warms, and hold the temperature of the grill to keep the stone at or around 500 degrees F.

USING PELLETS IN A PIZZA OVEN

Some dedicated pizza ovens are fueled by wood pellets, in addition to wood chunks or splits. This is not to be confused with using pellets in a pellet grill (such as Traeger). Each pizza oven manufacturer will have a different setup for how to insert the pellets. Start by following their instructions. To ignite the pellets, fill the pellet bin and then insert a tumbleweed fire starter into the center. Part of the starter should be sticking out. Light with matches or a torch and then set the pellets in the appropriate place. The pellets will ignite after 20 minutes.

Once the pellets are lit, continue to add small amounts of pellets while the fire is burning. Stay close to the pizza oven throughout this process because pellets burn quickly. You do not want the fire to go out, otherwise as you add pellets it will smother and create a dark creosote smoke. To avoid this, add small amounts of pellets as the fire is rolling.

Before cooking pizza we like to add a small handful of pellets to get the fire stoked and large enough to cook the top of the pizza. If you are using this type of pizza oven make sure to consult the manufacturer for best practices.

PROPANE

Propane provides a unique approach to managing heat. A gas grill can stay at a constant temperature, which keeps your pizza stone at a consistent temperature.

With a propane (or natural gas) pizza oven, such as the Gozney Dome or Ooni Karu multi-fuel, you can adjust the flame intensity as you put pizzas on and take them out.

1   Start a propane grill on a high flame to get the internal chamber and pizza stone to your desired temperature.

2   Once the oven, and more importantly the pizza stone, reaches its desired temperature, you can turn the flame down to maintain the heat. Then, just before you launch your pizza onto the stone, turn the flame back on high to create the convection current and heat to cook the top of the pizza while the stone cooks the bottom.

3   When your pizza is done, reduce the flame slightly to get the stone back to temp and repeat as needed.

CHEF'S TIP: When using propane for pizza, keep a second/backup tank full and ready to go when needed. Trust us when we say you don't want to be in the middle of an epic pizza night only to run out of fuel mid-party and have no backup. Talk about being a Debbie Downer!

SAFETY

It's important to highlight that live-fire cooking requires your full attention. Be sure that you don't leave fires unattended for a long period of time.

Grills and pizza ovens using charcoal and wood should be placed over a grill-safe mat, which prevents any fires if embers or charcoal fall out of the grill.

Always have a fire extinguisher available in case something unexpected happens.

To minimize the risk of grease fires, be sure your grill or oven is clean of any grease, ash, or prior spent fuel. Old fuel, especially if wet or ashy, will mute your fire and slow everything down when you are trying to reach your desired temperature.

Be sure to shut down your grill when you are done.

ADVERSE WEATHER

Don't let rain, wind, or snow prevent you from making awesome pizzas outside. Understand how the weather can affect your cooker and how the heat source works.

WIND. If the wind is blowing, rotate any pizza ovens so that the opening of the oven faces away from the direction of the wind. This keeps a propane flame from blowing out and allows for a more efficient airflow. When using wood, this positioning prevents the wood from getting too hot if the wind is constantly stoking the fire.

Plan an extra 15 minutes to get your heat source to the correct temperature in windy conditions.

RAIN. Rain is usually combined with higher humidity. Rain won't prevent you from cooking, but it can slow things down. For the best results, use your grill or oven under a cover or canopy. But if you don't have one, like us, then keep your wood or fuel source dry. Wet wood and charcoal are more difficult to ignite and keep hot. If it's a cold rain, add 15 extra minutes to your prep time to get your grill up to temperature. If your pizza stone is wet, it will take longer to warm up and release the moisture; try to keep the pizza oven covered in between use.

SUBFREEZING TEMPERATURE. Whether subfreezing temps or snow, cold weather slows down the entire cooking process. When heating up a grill or pizza oven, gradually warm up the pizza stone to prevent a thermal shock, which can cause a cracked stone or deck. We plan an hour in total to slowly bring our oven to temperature during very cold weather.

- **FIRST 20 MINUTES:** Start by bringing your fire to medium heat, or roughly 350 degrees F.
- **SECOND 20 MINUTES:** Bring your fire to medium-high heat, or roughly 500 degrees F.
- **THIRD 20 MINUTES:** If using a pizza oven, get it to 1,000 degrees F until the deck reads 700–725 degrees F. If using any cooker other than a pizza oven, wait until the stone reaches 500 degrees F.

Choosing a Pizza Cooker: Grill or Oven

GRILLS AND PIZZA OVENS

The goal of this section is to make sure we can meet you with the grill or pizza cooker you have, so the idea is to provide some additional specifics on how we set up and bake our pizzas on the most common types of grills and pizza ovens. From there, you can use the recipes in this book to make each type of pizza based on your setup.

If you want more details on the pros and cons of each grill and pizza oven, we have many articles on our website.

DOME VS STONE TEMPERATURE

Whenever we mention a dome thermometer temperature, as on a kettle grill or kamado, we are referring to the reading on the thermometer built into the lid of the grill. The dome temperature is not going to be the same as the stone temperature. This is why we mention the approximate temperature of the dome thermometer as well as the stone or steel temperature.

The most important temperature to follow when making pizza is that of the pizza stone, not the dome thermometer.

SMOKE/AIR EXITS

VENT

VENT

GRILL

COOL AIR COOL AIR

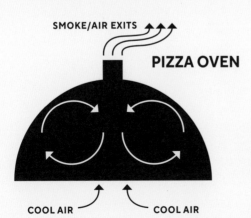

SMOKE/AIR EXITS

PIZZA OVEN

COOL AIR COOL AIR

KETTLE-STYLE GRILLS

These grills are the multi-tool of outdoor cooking. They allow for almost every technique, but the trade-off is that they aren't necessarily built to be great at any one thing (except hot and fast grilling).

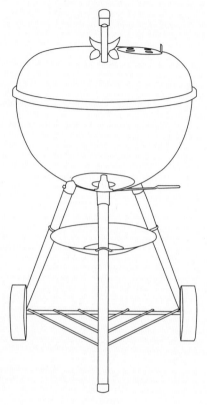

SETUP. Light the charcoal in a chimney. When it is lit and the entire chimney is a white ash, dump the charcoal around the outer edges of the grill. We call this "the doughnut method." Add fresh charcoal over the top following the same pattern. Then put your grill grate in place and the pizza steel on the center. (Imagine the shape of a doughnut, with the center being the steel and the doughnut being the charcoal ring.) Allow the steel to come to a temperature of 500 degrees F.

STEEL TEMPERATURE. The steel should be at 500 degrees F. Any hotter and the steel can burn the crust before the toppings are ready and the cheese is melted. A steel is not as forgiving as a stone, so we recommend being as precise as possible in maintaining the temperature at 500 degrees F.

We do not recommend a pizza stone for kettle grills because the heat source can get too hot and cause cracking. If all you have is a pizza stone, be sure your charcoal is set around the outer edge or to each side of the grill so it's not sitting directly under the pizza stone. Let us be your cautionary tale: save yourself the many stones we had to go through during testing.

COOKING. You do not need to rotate the pizza, as the convection is pretty even in a kettle grill. Allow the steel to come back up to temperature before placing the next pizza. If your pizza steel exceeds 550 degrees F, you run the risk of burning the bottom of your pizza before it's done, so be sure to carefully monitor the steel temp. If you have to, use high-heat gloves to remove the steel and cool it down.

COOKING TIME. Cooking times will average 8–10 minutes using a pizza steel.

BIG GREEN EGG AND KAMADO GRILLS

Big Green Eggs and the similarly styled kamado grills are some of the best and most efficient grills for all types of cooking styles—from baking to hot and fast grilling, smoking, and of course, making pizzas. There are now many accessories in addition to pizza stones, like the Big Green Egg Pizza Oven attachment, that allows it to mimic a pizza oven.

TRADITIONAL PIZZA STONE SETUP. Light the charcoal and place the ConvEGGtor or heat plate over it with the legs facing up. Set the grate on the heat plate and then the pizza stone on the grate. Open vents wide and allow the grill to reach 500 degrees F as read in the dome thermometer. As the temperature of the grill rises, occasionally check the pizza stone temperature. If the stone reaches 500 degrees F before the dome thermometer, start to close off part of your vents to maintain the current heat and hold the stone at 500–550 degrees F. The dome thermometer will read between 500 and 550 degrees. Unlike other grills, kamado grills are so efficient that the hot air may be warmer on the stone than in the dome thermometer.

HOW IT WORKS. Kamado grills are designed for incredible efficiency in heat and convection currents. The vents are designed so that air enters from the bottom vent, fans the fire (and heat), and then escapes through the top vent while curling over the upper portion of the cooking chamber.

STONE TEMPERATURE. Should be 500–550 degrees F. Do not let the stone exceed 550 degrees F, or you will run the risk of burning the bottom of the pizza crust.

COOKING. Due to vent placements, the hotter portion of the Big Green Egg is toward the back hinges. So it's important to rotate your pizza at least once, using a turning peel for a more even cook on the crust. Allow the pizza stone to come back up in temperature before adding your next pizza.

PIZZA OVEN WEDGE ACCESSORY. Follow the same setup procedure for the traditional pizza stone. Place the wedge onto the base of the Egg, and close the top lid so it aligns with the wedge. Bring the pizza stone to 500 degrees F. Follow the same instructions.

COOKING TIME. Cooking times will average 8–12 minutes.

CHEF'S TIP: If you are cooking a lot of pizzas, you may need a refuel. Minimize how long your Egg is open so that you can better control the heat. If you refuel, it will immediately cool your heat source and decrease your grill temperature by half. You will need to plan time to allow the grill to return to temperature.

PELLET GRILLS

Pellet grills are great because they are easy to set and hold specific temperatures. The downside is that many don't exceed 500 degrees F on a high grill mode.

HOW IT WORKS. Wood pellets are fed to a heat source. The hotter you want the pellet grill, the faster the pellets are added to the fire. A fan stokes the fire and pushes the heat through the pellet grill via convection. The hottest part of a pellet grill is the upper portion of the chamber because the fan forces hot air to the top of the grill and then down. For this reason, we recommend raising your pizza stone in a pellet grill higher off the lowest grate. If you don't have multiple grates, you can buy an accessory to give the stone some lift to maximize that higher heat.

SETUP. Be sure the deflector plate is installed and the pellet hopper is full. Turn on your pellet grill to its highest setting. If you have multiple racks in your pellet grill, use the highest one that will fit your pizza stone. Allow the stone to reach 500 degrees F. If it won't exceed 450 degrees F (which is common on many pellet grills), then just plan more time for the pizza to cook.

COOKING. Like any convection oven, we like to rotate the pizza halfway through the cooking process for even cooking.

COOKING TIME. Cooking times will average 12–14 minutes if your grill is under 500 degrees F, and 10–12 minutes if it exceeds 500 degrees F.

GAS GRILLS

Gas grills can also make some delicious outdoor pizzas. They can handle a pizza stone or a steel. If you have three or more burners, use a stone. If you have one or two burners, use a steel. The direct heat on smaller gas grills can crack a pizza stone. The downside is that they aren't great at providing convection heat, so the pizzas may take longer to cook. Additionally, the edges of the crust don't achieve the same level of browning as a typical crust because it's not getting that top heat source, so don't expect them to look the same as a pizza fresh out of a pizza oven. Gas grills will vary in size. The following guide focuses on a three-burner model.

HOW IT WORKS. Gas grills are similar to your kitchen oven. They have a heat source fed by the propane in a large cooking chamber. Gas grills don't offer as much even convection currents, so you need to make sure the flame is high and the stone stays hot.

SETUP. Set the two outer burners to medium-high heat. Place the pizza stone in the center of the grill (over the burner that is not lit). Allow the internal temperature of the grill to reach 550–600 degrees F, then measure the temperature of the stone. Adjust the propane levels to maintain the stone temperature.

STONE TEMPERATURE. Should be 500–550 degrees F.

COOKING. Since gas grills have uneven heat distribution, be sure to rotate the pizza on the stone 180 degrees midway through the cooking process for an even cook. If you have shelves and can manage to elevate your pizza stone safely, it will be hotter on the upper portion of the grill.

COOKING TIME. Expect an average of 10–14 minutes to cook, depending on the size of the pizza.

PIZZA OVENS

Pizza ovens are engineered with a high-heat pizza stone, called a deck, and an area for the heat source, whether that's a propane burner or a large enough space for a wood fire. They are able to reach internal temperatures of 700–1,000 degrees F, which allow for Neapolitan-style pizzas. They can also bake with the right cast-iron dishes, making them a versatile outdoor oven.

HOW IT WORKS. The embers (or propane flame) keep the cooking area hot, including the pizza deck. The deck cooks the crust while the embers bake the sides of the pizza. To get the right level of heat over the top, you want a rolling flame across the ceiling of the oven. This directs heat to the toppings, helps melt the cheese, and cooks the top at the same time as the base. These three factors allow the pizzas to cook quickly, evenly, and efficiently.

It's important to preheat your wood-fired pizza oven for at least 30 minutes so that your pizza stone is hot all the way through. Remember what we said about the kids' pizza. The larger your pizza oven, the longer it will take to heat up.

USING WOOD. Set up your wood splits like a log cabin in the center of your pizza oven, and place a tumbleweed fire starter in the center. Light it, and allow the wood to ignite. Continue to add wood to build an ember base for 15 minutes. Then move the wood to the side of your oven, and continue to feed the fire until the stone reads between 700 and 750 degrees F. The internal temperature of the oven will hover near 900 degrees F.

USING PROPANE. When using propane, ignite the fuel and turn on a high setting to warm up the oven and the stone. During cold weather, follow our subfreezing-temperature startup process on page 24. When cooking pizzas, as you are heating the oven, lower the propane flame slightly just as the stone reaches your desired temperature. This will keep it from getting too hot. Then, right when you're about to make a pizza, turn up the propane flame and leave it up (hot) while the pizza is cooking. It's about regulating the heat, not letting it get too hot or too cool. Think about it like managing the flame on a gas burner on your stovetop. You have that same kind of control over the heat source when using propane on a pizza oven.

COOKING. When the deck has come to temperature, and before adding your pizza, be sure there is a rolling flame over the ceiling of the unit. It should have a continuous rolling flame when cooking the pizza. When we are only using wood, we like to maintain a hot ember base at all times. Then, minutes before we place our pizza, we add a fresh piece of wood. This creates a rolling flame while baking your pizza, allowing for even cooking on the crust and toppings. When using propane, we turn up the flame to high when we launch the pizza into the oven.

OVEN MODIFICATION

If all you have is your kitchen oven, have no fear. The best way to work with your oven for Neapolitan-style pizza is to use a pizza stone set in the middle rack. Turn your oven on as hot as it will go. We recommend 550 degrees F. Let the pizza stone preheat for at least 30 minutes, ideally an hour. The entire stone should be radiating serious heat, with a temperature reading of about 550 degrees F. Then add your pizza. Cook for 4 minutes and then rotate it. Turn on the broiler and cook for an additional 2–4 minutes, or until the top is browned and the dough is cooked through. Adjust times as not all ovens have the same heat level. Once the broiler is on, do not walk away from the pizza.

TURNING PIZZA. When using a pizza oven, it's important to rotate the pizza using a turning peel. This allows for even cooking along the edges of the crust because the flame is typically isolated to one small area of your oven. The hotter you are cooking the pizza, the faster you will need to rotate it. In general, we rotate the pizza four times, one rotation every 20 seconds or so. It's important that you never leave the pizza unattended once it's launched. You can rotate as you see the crust rise and brown since every flame will be a little different on every cook.

STONE TEMPERATURE. Should be 700–750 degrees F for Neapolitan-style pizzas, 550 degrees F for New York–style pizzas and baking.

CHEF'S TIP: Sometimes the toppings need a little extra time to bake when the crust sides and bottom are done. If this is the case, we will place the pizza peel under the pizza and lift it several inches closer to the lid (top) to get intense heat for only a couple of seconds. Just a mere couple of seconds under that heat should finish cooking the cheese and toppings.

COOKING TIME. For Neapolitan-style pizzas, expect 90 seconds for the pizza to be done after consistently rotating it. For New York–style pizzas, expect them to be done at the lower heat and turning at 5–7 minutes. You will need to turn New York–style pizzas more often to avoid burning the crust.

PARBAKING

This is a useful technique if you don't have a stone, steel, or dedicated pizza oven. Parbaking involves pre-grilling your dough before adding any toppings. This allows the dough to firm up, creating a sturdy base to hold the toppings. It's more akin to flatbread-style dishes. If you don't have a pizza stone, then modify any of the recipes in this book by parbaking the dough. With dedicated pizza ovens, you don't need to parbake.

1   It's best to parcook the dough using indirect heat, or lower the target temperature of the grill to 400 degrees F.
2   Place the shaped dough directly onto the grill grates.
3   Cook for 2 minutes, or until you see some grill marks develop.
4   Flip for an additional minute and then remove. Add your toppings and place back on the grill to finish.

CHEF'S TIP: If parbaking, use a low-hydration dough (see Dough chapter, page 93) so it won't fall through the grates. You can even split the dough in half to create smaller and easier-to-manage grilled pizzas. If you're parbaking multiple pizzas, form the pizza rounds and parbake all of them first. Then turn up the heat, add toppings, and finish the pizzas at the recommended temperatures.

WINE

CANTINA DI
SOLIERA
CANTINA DI
SOLIERA
LAMBRUSCO
DI SORBARA
2022

PIZZA IS THE QUINTESSENTIAL CASUAL COMFORT FOOD. It's the ultimate Friday night dinner at the end of a busy week. It's something that we—adults, kids, picky eaters, vegetarians, and carnivores alike—can all agree on. And while there are few components to pizza that scream upscale or fancy, that doesn't mean you can't enjoy a nice glass of wine with your pie.

Wine is our drink of choice for pizza night. While for many beer seems to be the preferred beverage to enjoy with pizza, we find it fills us up more quickly than wine, leaving less room for the array of delicious pizzas on the evening lineup. So wine it is.

But if you're not a wine drinker at all, then this book is still for you! As in our previous book, *Fire + Wine,* the wine plays a small yet important role. It's there to enhance and elevate the experience for those who choose it. Wine was made for food, and in many ways food was made for wine. The recipes and techniques are still the stars of this book, and wine is a supporting character. Like our first book, you don't need to drink anything to enjoy the forty-plus recipes covered herein. But if you happen to be wine curious and getting a little thirsty, read on.

Similar to *Fire + Wine,* the goal of this chapter is to provide a basic understanding of how food and wine pairings work, and how these principles apply to the pizza recipes in this cookbook. We are restating some of the information from our previous book because the fundamentals of pairing wine with food—whether the cuisine be BBQ or pizza (or any others)—generally stay the same. While the flavors and techniques change, the guidelines can be applied for all styles of food.

So even if you read our first book, we still encourage you to read this chapter to understand how it applies to pizza.

There is no such thing as a "perfect pairing." To imply something is *perfect,* means it cannot be topped, it is without fault, unequivocally flawless. That is impossible to achieve with something as subjective as taste.

There are no two people who taste things the exact same, so what may be perfect to us may not be perfect to you. We can go on and on about how amazing our mushroom pizza is with this bottle of pinot noir, but if you're just not a pinot noir fan, the pairing won't work for you, and there is nothing we can do to convince you otherwise. Period. There's nothing wrong with the pairing; it's just not for you. And that's okay!

If you search the internet for the best wine for a pepperoni pizza, you will probably get about a thousand completely different answers. In this book, we offer some fun recommendations based on our experience and research, so you can apply these guidelines to finding your own ultimate pairing.

The "Rules" of Food and Wine Pairing

We always like to start by reminding people that the number one "rule" of food and wine pairing is to "ignore the rules and drink what you like." While that statement is absolutely true (it is certainly important that you enjoy the wine in your glass), we believe there are some basic factors that can give you a base to understand an intricate subject without overthinking or oversimplifying it.

Wine is meant to be fun and enjoyable, not intimidating or rigid. Don't let anyone tell you otherwise. So let's toss the idea that there are any official rules to pairing wine with food. Instead, I want to remind

you of the recommendations that will help you get the most out of any dining experience involving wine. Recommendations are just that: a suggestion you can choose to follow or not. Who knows, maybe you'll even have an aha moment with a pairing that may just be perfect for *you.*

Our goal for any pairing is to create *balance.* The food should not overpower the wine, nor should the wine overpower the food. It's the same idea for food. Food should be a balance of flavors, not any one thing, or it throws off the taste experience.

Pay attention to the following elements of food and wine, especially how they apply to pizza.

COMPLEMENTARY FLAVORS

The taste of the food and wine being consumed together should be similar. A sauce shouldn't be sweeter than the wine. Acid in a dish should be sufficiently matched to the acid levels in the wine. When it comes to the pizza sauces in this book, most are considered just one of many layers in the overall experience. Apply the sauces sparingly or in a way that the sauce will be in balance with any additional toppings and cheese. The pizza sauce shouldn't be the dominant flavor.

CONTRASTING FLAVORS

Opposites attract. Match up contrasting flavors, such as sweet wine with a salty or spicy dish. Or even a light, high-acid wine with a rich, fatty dish. This is going to apply to a few recipes in this book where the dish may be slightly spicy; we will tame that spice with a slightly sweet-style wine, creating synergy.

BODY AND WEIGHT

The weight of a dish should be matched by the weight of the wine.

When it comes to detecting the weight in wine, the best analogy we've heard is to compare skim milk to whole milk and heavy cream. Skim milk is light on the palate. The more you move toward cream, the heavier it feels on your palate. Light-bodied wines, like pinot gris for example, feel more like skim milk, whereas full-bodied wines, like syrah or zinfandel, are closer to that whole-milk feel. Both white and red wines can fit into both categories, light-bodied and full-bodied.

In general, the body and weight of most pizza recipes in this book will be the same. It's not like comparing a rich braised beef stew with a grilled chicken breast.

Fundamental Elements of Wine and Food Pairing

ACIDITY

Acid is one of the most important factors to consider, and it is found in both food and wine. It's what keeps a wine lively on the palate and gives it an innate ability to pair with food because it acts as a palate cleanser. Good acidity in wine can be detected by a sharpness or jolt, usually near the front of your tongue, followed by your mouth starting to water. In general, the more your mouth begins to water, the higher the acidity.

When it comes to pairing, the acidity of a dish should be matched by the acidity in the wine. This can be hard to detect, we know.

If the food is more acidic than the wine, then the wine will taste flabby or flat. Think about what happens to soda when the carbonation wears off—it gets flat, uninteresting, and all you taste is the sugar. Want to test this concept? Try tasting a salad with a lemon- and vinegar-based dressing (two ingredients that are very high in acidity) paired with a viognier or an oaked chardonnay from a warmer region in California. The wine, which has much less acidity than the dressing, will taste unbalanced and flat paired with the high-acid dish. However, with a high-acid wine, like sauvignon blanc, it can sing.

Consider the pairing of Chianti (an Italian region and high-acid wine made from sangiovese grapes) with a pizza made with a simple tomato sauce (like on page 107). Tomatoes are high in acid and the sauce is usually medium–heavy bodied. Both go well with a wine that is matched in weight and also high in acid.

Generally speaking, wines from cooler climates tend to display higher levels of acidity. Wines that are high in acid include (but are not limited to) sparkling wine, sauvignon blanc, riesling, albariño, pinot gris/grigio, sangiovese, barbera, gamay, and pinot noir.

Acid in Pizza

Similarly, acid pops up in pizza with tomato-based sauces, pesto, and pickled toppings.

Take the Diavola on page 151, for example. It starts with an acidic tomato base, and is then layered with three acidic meats and topped with spicy pickled peppers. That acid shows up on the sides of your tongue with a tangy sensation, making your mouth water. Therefore, you want a wine that matches and balances that acidity while also refreshing your palate, such as a fruity, vibrant rosé.

Acid in wine is important as a counterpoint to rich, salty, or fatty foods. If you are looking to "cut" a dish that has these qualities, seek a wine with good acid. Think the Biscuits and Gravy Pizza on page 183, featuring a rich gravy and fatty sausage, or the Goat Cheese and Mushroom Pizza with creamy white sauce on page 139. Both are great

A PINK PARTY: WHAT TO KNOW ABOUT ROSÉ

Rosé wines are generally produced from red grapes. When grapes are pressed (prior to fermentation), the juices of nearly every single grape variety run clear. It's the skins that give wine its color. For red wines, the grapes are pressed and fermented with their skins attached. For white wines, the skins are removed prior to fermentation, leaving that pure juice and clear color. For rosé, the red grapes are pressed and will spend some amount of time (from a few hours to 12 or more) soaking with the skins, imparting some color before the juices are separated from the skins.

Saignée, or "bleeding," is another method whereby, similar to the process

matches for something light and bubbly, like sparkling wine, to help refresh your palate after a bite of richly textured pizza.

SWEETNESS

In wine, the sweet taste is residual sugar (sugar left after fermentation) that remains in the wine. Quite often it is confused for fruity characteristics that may have zero residual sugar. Lots of fruit aromatics can come across as "sweet" even though a wine could be technically "dry."

The golden rule of sweet foods and wine is that the sweetness of a dish should be matched or exceeded by the sweetness of the wine (a dry wine would taste sour and unpleasant). When it comes to pairing sweet flavors, understand that sweetness reduces perception of sweetness. What do we mean by that? When you taste a sweet wine paired with an equally sweet dish, you notice the perceived sweetness less. When paired correctly, they balance each other out, creating harmony.

This can be hard to detect, especially in desserts, which is why pairing wine and chocolate can be tricky, but not impossible! Sweet wines also pair well with contrasting flavors, like spicy food. This is because

described above, the grapes will sit in their skins, allowing some of the juices to "bleed" off into a new vat in order to produce a rosé. What remains of the red juice will be more concentrated and intense.

In some examples, rosé can be made from blending finished red wine and white together (this is common with rosé sparkling wine), but the best styles are produced from the maceration method mentioned above.

Rosés range from light, crisp, and bright, to dark, intense, and deeply fruity. You may also see some labeled Blush or White Zinfandel, and these can be intensely sweet. The wines recommended in this book lean toward the dry style, as we find them more refreshing and better suited to our recipes.

sweet wines can help to cool and refresh the palate after a bite of something with a spicy kick to it. Riesling is an example of a wine that can be sweet. More and more riesling wines will have a useful scale on the back of the label indicating the sweetness level of the wine.

If a wine is described as "dry," then it usually has zero or very little residual sugar (or sweetness) to it.

Sweetness in Pizza

If you use the tomato sauce recipes in this book, they shouldn't taste very sweet. Unlike many store-bought pizza sauces, we don't add sugar to ours.

While we have some perceptually sweet flavors in some of the sauces and recipes, we hope that you'll find they are balanced out with the savory toppings and salty cheeses. There are a few sweet dessert dishes, and we've done our best to pair them with wines using the tools in this chapter.

So don't be afraid of the seemingly sweet-looking recipes in this book. Our dishes are intended to be a balance of sweet, spicy, and savory. And like a well-made wine, not one element should dominate or stand out too much. And a dessert wine is great on occasion, just like a dessert pizza.

TANNIN

Tannin in wine comes from two different sources: the skins and seeds of the grapes and wood tannins from oak barrel aging. Tannins are most commonly found in red wines (though they can be detected in whites as well).

Tannin is best described by the sensation it leaves in your mouth, which can be bitter and dry, astringent, and gritty. Picture unsweetened tea that has been steeped too long. The dry, gritty feeling that overcomes your tongue is from the tannins. Tannins tend to soften and mellow out with age. When it comes to pairing wines high in tannin with food, here are a few factors to consider:

- **FAT AND PROTEIN REDUCE PERCEPTION OF TANNIN.** This is why red meat and young cabernet sauvignon go so well together. The protein and fat in the beef soften the mouth-drying tannins from the wine.
- **SALT ALSO REDUCES PERCEPTION OF TANNIN.** Try melting salty blue cheese over pizza and pairing it with a cabernet sauvignon or a tempranillo from Spain's Rioja or Ribera del Duero regions. That saltiness from the cheese minimizes the otherwise noticeable tannins in the wine. It's also just a delicious combination. You can see an example of this pairing on page 153 with the Date-Night Steak Dinner Pizza.

ALCOHOL

Alcohol is the result of fermentation: the biological process that converts sugars (naturally found in grapes) into energy, producing ethanol (alcohol) and carbon dioxide as by-products. The amount of alcohol in wine will be based on various factors, such as how much sugar the grapes had to begin with prior to fermentation. Alcohol in wine ranges from around 9 percent ABV (alcohol by volume) on the very low end, to 15 percent on the high end, with the majority of wines in the 12–14 percent range.

When pairing food with alcohol, consider the following:

- **ALCOHOL ACCENTUATES HEAT.** Try tasting a high-alcohol wine, like a zinfandel, that has more than 15 percent ABV with a really spicy dish. Everything, both the wine and the dish, will taste hotter (the food will seem spicier, and the wine will seem more alcoholic). It's best to serve spicy dishes with a medium- to low-alcoholic wine, or contrast it with a wine that is slightly sweet and refreshing to cool and cleanse the palate. This is why beer and hot wings are a match made in heaven. But, of course, this book isn't about beer. Or wings. Though, now that we think of it, a hot-wing pizza suddenly sounds delicious!

- **ALCOHOL IS ACCENTUATED BY SALT AND PEPPER.** This is important to consider with ingredients like pepperoni (or other cured meats) and some cheeses, like Parmesan or pecorino, which can be on the salty side. Too much salt in a dish will make a wine seem "hot," or more alcoholic. Balance those flavors with lower-alcohol wines.

OAK IN WINE

Most red wines and some white (many chardonnays in particular) are fermented and/or aged in oak barrels, often imparting subtle vanilla, caramel, oak, toast, char, or smoky characteristics to the wines. As previously mentioned, oak can also transmit tannins to wines. While oak can be a distracting factor in pairing with some cuisines, the flavors that result from oak can be quite complementary to grilled and smoked foods.

Cooking Methods and Ingredients

Cooking methods, from sautéing to grilling or smoking, will alter the flavor of any given food and its resulting wine pairing. The two styles of cooking described throughout this book are grilling over charcoal and in hot wood-fired/propane pizza ovens (as explained in the Fire chapter, page 11). The grilled pizzas will come across as more smoky versus those cooked in a dedicated pizza oven fueled by propane.

SAUCES, INGREDIENTS, AND STYLES TO CONSIDER

When it comes to pizza, sauces and dominant ingredients change all the so-called rules and will ultimately determine the wine recommendations. Sauces can be the base to a pizza, from pesto to tomato-based sauces, to dressings on a salad pizza, to finishing glazes (like some hot honey or balsamic vinegar).

With some of these classic pizza combinations, keep these factors in mind and match the dominant sauce with the intended wine.

SIMPLE TOMATO SAUCE: The base for a simple Margherita pizza. The simplicity and elegance of this sauce calls for a wine that's equally refined. Chianti Classico (made predominantly from sangiovese grapes) works great here. Other lightweight reds pair equally well, like pinot noir, Beaujolais (made from gamay noir grapes), or Italian barbera.

PESTO: With its bold basil and salty taste, pesto is a flavor explosion. The zesty, herbaceous qualities of a sauvignon blanc beautifully mirror the basil in the pesto. Its crisp acidity and bright citrus notes provide a refreshing contrast to the richness of the cheese, creating a lively and invigorating pairing.

WHITE SAUCE: For a white sauce, which contains dairy products, pair with a wine with good acidity to create a sense of balance with the fat and richness found in dairy. The vibrant bubbles in sparkling wines work perfectly here to cut through the richness of the creamy slice. Plus, everything is better with bubbles! Other excellent candidates include pinot gris, sauvignon blanc, and other zesty white wines.

PEPPERONI OR SPICY CURED MEATS: The herb- and spice-seasoned meats have a strong pepper, anise, garlic, and fennel flavor. There's also the admittedly irresistible oil that those cured meats release as they cook that begs for a wine with some tannic structure to balance out that fat and intensity, and stand up to those flavors. Syrah is a great partner, as are other bold reds with robust tannins and dark berry flavors.

MUSHROOMS: Pizzas laden with earthy mushrooms call for a wine that can match that depth of flavor. The delicate yet complex nature of a pinot noir is a wonderful complement to the earthiness of mushrooms. Pinot's natural high acid also balances out the umami flavor of the mushrooms and brightens it up with its innate red berry fruit notes.

ROASTED OR GRILLED VEGETABLES: Loading up a pie with veggies calls for a fuller-bodied white wine, like chardonnay or chenin blanc. The grape's ripe stone fruit and honey notes are strong enough to handle any bold flavors from vegetables. For those topped with arugula, grüner veltliner is a fun match.

BREAKFAST PIZZAS: These come in a variety of flavors and styles, but may contain an element of meat (think breakfast sausage or ham for a Benedict) with a cracked egg over the top. Nothing screams brunch more than sparkling wine. The bubbles will cut through the richness of the egg. And, let's be honest, no brunch is complete without celebratory bubbly.

DESSERT PIZZAS: Dessert pizzas can be adorned with chocolate, fruit, and perhaps a dusting of powdered sugar, as a gratifying way to end a meal. Depending on what the star of the pizza is, you'll want to find a wine that can stand up to the sweetness of the pie. Most still wines will fall short on the sweetness factor. But there are other options! The luscious, fruity sweetness of a ruby port complements the dessert pizza's sugary elements. Its velvety texture and notes of ripe berries create a heavenly combination that's akin to a berry compote drizzled over a chocolaty crust. For the fruit pizzas, perhaps with some mascarpone or creamy element, go with a sweeter sparkling wine or riesling.

The Wines and Styles Chosen for This Book

There are thousands of grapes in existence that have been used to make wine. Jancis Robinson, one of the world's renowned wine writers, published a book detailing 1,368 of them! And around 150 of those are commercially produced throughout the world.

For the purpose of this book, the grapes we have chosen to pair with these pizza recipes are considered classic, international, or noble. They are grapes that have become household names and have worldwide recognition and widespread consumer appeal. These are grapes that are widely planted, which you're likely to encounter at most wine shops or at your supermarket.

We also reference some popular regional wines and blends (like Rioja, Bordeaux, and Côtes du Rhône) because, although they may

RED WINES

Barbera	Medium-bodied	Fruity. Cherry, strawberry, plum, violet, lavender
Cabernet Franc	Medium- to full-bodied	Herbaceous. Plum, strawberry, black cherry, roasted bell pepper, chili pepper
Cabernet Sauvignon	Full-bodied	Black currant, black cherry, blueberry, cassis, eucalyptus, oak, baking spice
Carménère	Medium-bodied	Green bell pepper, plum, raspberry, cherry, blackberry, spice, dark cocoa, leather
Gamay	Light-bodied	Bright, floral, fruity. Raspberry, violet, black currant, tart cherry
Grenache	Medium-bodied	Wide range based on region. Strawberry, raspberry, black cherry, tobacco, white pepper
Malbec	Medium- to full-bodied	Smoky. Dry and plump dark fruit, black cherry, plum, raspberry, blackberry
Merlot	Medium- to full-bodied	Blackberry, plum, chocolate, vanilla
Mourvèdre	Full-bodied	Dark color, dry, rich, and spicy. Plum, blackberry, blueberry, black pepper, violet
Petite Sirah	Full-bodied	Big, powerful, tannic, and dense. Plum, blueberry, chocolate, black pepper, blackberry, licorice, allspice
Pinot Noir	Light- to medium-bodied	Ranging from earthy to fruity. Cherry, cranberry, strawberry, rose, rhubarb, mushroom
Sangiovese	Light- to medium-bodied	Fruity, acidic. Cherry, plum, roasted pepper, tomato, herbs (like sage and thyme)
Syrah	Full-bodied	Meaty. Ground white and black pepper, baking spice, cured meat, blackberry, blueberry, plum, violet
Tempranillo	Full-bodied	Can be dry and big with high tannins and acidity. Cherry, plum, tobacco, fig, vanilla, leather
Zinfandel	Full-bodied	Plum, jam, blackberry, black cherry, tobacco

WHITE WINES

Albariño	Light- to medium-bodied	Zesty. Citrus, grapefruit, apricot, honeydew, pear
Arneis	Light- to medium-bodied	Dry, floral, fruity, nutty. Peach, apple, honey, apricot
Chardonnay	Medium- to full-bodied	Wide range from crisp to buttery and creamy. Apple, pear, citrus, pineapple, vanilla, caramel
Chenin Blanc	Light-bodied	Dry to off-dry. Apple, lemon, pear
Grüner Veltliner	Medium-bodied	Herbaceous. Apple, peach, citrus, mineral, white pepper
Pinot Blanc	Medium-bodied	Herbal, spicy, crisp. Green apple, citrus
Pinot Gris/Grigio	Light-bodied	Crisp, fruity. Pear, peach, apricot, apple, citrus, melon
Riesling	Light-bodied	Ranging from crisp and dry to sweet. Apricot, apple, lemon, peach, nectarine, honeysuckle
Rosé	Light- to medium-bodied	Crisp, fruity. Red berry fruit and citrus
Sauvignon Blanc	Light-bodied	Herbaceous, grassy. Citrus (such as grapefruit), pineapple, peach
Sparkling	Light-bodied	Crisp. Apple, pear, bread, yeast
Torrontés	Medium-bodied	Dry and aromatic. Lemon, peach, flower/rose petals
Verdicchio	Light-bodied	Acidic, crisp, zesty. Citrus and peach aromas
Vermentino	Light- to medium-bodied	Round, fruity. Green apple, pear, citrus, grapefruit, almond
Viognier	Full-bodied	Floral, fruity, creamy. Apricot, pear, peach, honeysuckle

not be single varietal wines, they are great for some of the dishes presented here and worth seeking out, and are very distinct from their counterparts in other parts of the world. So there are times when we specify which wine region is best for a certain dish.

And since Italy is the birthplace of modern pizza, we have included a few lesser-known, but equally if not more delicious, Italian wines for good measure.

LET'S GET BUBBLY

Champagne is truly Mary's favorite beverage in the world. But let's be clear on one thing, true Champagne only comes from the Champagne region of northeast France. The word *champagne* has become synonymous with all things sparkling wine. But there's a big difference between the sparkling wine produced in this region of France and those produced elsewhere.

So what is champagne, then?

Champagne is produced by a process referred to as *méthode traditionnelle* (or *méthode champenoise*), when, after primary fermentation (the fermentation that converts sugar to alcohol), the wines go through a secondary fermentation in the bottle. The then-still wine is placed into a bottle, along with a small amount of yeast and sugar, initiating a second fermentation. This step creates carbon dioxide, which forms the bubbles, or effervescence, once the bottle is opened.

Even within France, but outside the Champagne region, you'll find sparkling wines labeled Crémant: Crémant de Bourgogne (sparkling wines from Burgundy), Crémant de Loire (sparkling wines from the Loire region), and so forth. These are made using the méthode traditionnelle and can be quite delicious, but they are not Champagne.

In Spain, you'll find fruity and crisp sparkling wines labeled cava. These can be great values. Prosecco from Italy is sparkling wine produced in the Charmat method, where the bubbles are generated inside a large pressurized tank (versus inside the bottle). Lambrusco, also from Italy, is another bubbly mentioned a few times in this book. These tend to be light, sparkling red wines, ranging from dry to sweet, with cherry, strawberry, and raspberry notes.

Sparkling wines are commonly made by using the méthode traditionnelle throughout the world. A small number of wine producers are also carbonating their wines, which can help to keep costs down, but the quality of the bubbles is often sacrificed.

Sparkling wines are fantastic food-pairing wines and are recommended throughout the book. These wines aren't just for celebrations or aperitifs. These can and should be dinner wines as well, and we hope you're motivated to try some with your next pizza!

You can't write a book about backyard parties without mentioning rosé—the quintessential summer drink. And since sparkling wine is our all-time favorite style, it most certainly plays a central pairing role here as well. Plus, it's great with pizza!

Specific producers and vintages are not mentioned, but rather general regions, varietals, and styles that would pair with the recipes in this book.

It's also important to understand that the same grapes cultivated in different parts of the world can have extremely varied characteristics. Heck, grapes grown in the exact same region, a mile apart, can taste vastly different. So if we recommend a sauvignon blanc for a dish, understand that a bottle from New Zealand will taste different than one from the Loire region of France or California. The recommendations are meant to be a starting point. These are general guidelines. There will always be exceptions to every rule, every grape, every region!

And while Italy should get top honors for creating this pizza craze we all love, we can't limit the pairings to just Italian wines. There is a world of great wine out there, and we encourage you to explore it. A good wine shop can be an invaluable resource to finding the right bottles to pair with the recipes herein.

Food and wine pairing is a different experience for everyone! These pairings may not always work based on your personal preferences, but hopefully you'll develop the tools to understand the recipe elements and how they may react to your potential wines. You can make adjustments to the food based on your pairing.

Now, let's get the pizza party started!

REGIONS OR BLENDS MENTIONED IN THIS BOOK

- Beaujolais
- Bordeaux and blends
- Chianti
- Rhône style (whites and reds)
- Rioja

TOOLS + INGREDIENTS

When it comes to making pizza, there are an infinite number of tools you can buy. Many of them are fun to have, but a few are absolutely critical to making the best pizza possible. We break this down into two categories: must-have and nice-to-have.

Must-Have Tools

You have already read about the importance of the temperature of your pizza stone or steel. In order to measure that properly, you must have a good infrared (IR) thermometer.

IR THERMOMETER. The IR thermometer sends a beam to a fixed item and returns the surface temperature. This is critical for reading the pizza stone or steel for the optimal temperature. You do not want to rely on a dome thermometer to accurately reflect your actual pizza stone or steel temp. Don't use an IR thermometer to measure a flame, though; it's meant to read a solid-state object, and most won't measure more than 1,200 degrees F.

DIGITAL SCALE. The difference between good and great dough is in grams. A proper digital scale allows you the precision to weigh the ingredients so that your ratios for fermentation are as accurate as possible versus using measuring cups and spoons. A decent scale won't break the bank, but a poorly measured dough will break a few hearts. Okay, so that might not be true, but it will make for a poor pizza experience.

LARGE BOWLS. Preparing dough for fermentation requires getting your hands dirty and moving the dough and water around. A large stainless steel bowl makes the work so much easier and avoids spilling any of the precious ingredients. The bowl can also be used for fermentation as the dough rises. We use 13-inch-wide stainless steel prep bowls, which you can find at any restaurant supply store for cheap.

DOUGH SCRAPER. This is also called a bench scraper. Some would argue this is a nice-to-have, but we find a good dough scraper makes for better accuracy and cleanup, which turns it into an essential tool. You use it when prepping dough and when making pizza. And with twin boys in tow and a neighborhood of friends coming over on pizza night, that cleanup savings is worth every penny, but maybe that's just us.

WOODEN OR PLASTIC CUTTING BOARD. Using a large wooden cutting board allows more control when kneading and prepping dough. It doubles as a great prep space when making the pizzas and allows for easy cleanup. It's also much cheaper than marble or marble stone slabs, which many chefs prefer because the stone stays cool.

HALF SHEET PAN. When your dough is done rising and you are cutting it into smaller balls, having a half sheet pan is important so that they can continue to rise.

PLASTIC WRAP. You will use a lot of plastic wrap to keep your containers airtight. Buy the good stuff restaurants use, which is generally more clingy. If you are sustainably minded, we recommend using proofing boxes with kitchen towels. The proofing boxes have covers, and you can enhance the seal with a large kitchen towel without the need for plastic wrap. If freezing dough, you may want to use quart-sized plastic containers as an alternative to plastic wrap.

STAND MIXERS

We prefer to make our dough by hand straight out of the bowl. It is just as fast for us to make as using a stand mixer. But if you are preparing a lot of dough, feel free to use a stand mixer. For the best results, use the dough hook attachment, which will integrate all the flour and form the dough ball. We still recommend some manual kneading as well.

PIZZA STONE. A good pizza stone is critical if you don't have a dedicated pizza oven with an embedded stone. For grills, we recommend a stone at least 12 inches in diameter. Be sure it's not wider than your grill grates. We prefer a circular stone because most grills are circular (as are pizzas). If you have space for a square, that will provide you more cooking surface. Just be sure that the area of a square stone does not exceed the grill's diameter. Ideally, you want at least an inch of space between the stone and the edge of the grill to allow for convection airflow.

WHEN SOURCING YOUR PIZZA STONE, PAY CLOSE ATTENTION TO THE DETAILS. Any decent stone should be rated to more than 1,000 degrees F, ideally 1,400 degrees F. If it isn't rated, you run the risk of buying a stone meant for kitchen ovens that may crack due to the higher heat produced by charcoal.

PIZZA STEELS. These are a good investment if you have a grill that is better suited for direct cooking, such as a kettle-style grill. Steels won't crack from the direct heat, but they also get hot fast and can overshoot temperature. For kettle grills, we recommend placing the pizza steel over the stone because of the higher direct-heat potential.

PIZZA STONE VS PIZZA STEEL

Pizza stones provide ongoing radiant heat longer than a steel. Pizza steels can handle direct heat better than a stone. We recommend a high-heat-rated pizza stone unless you are using a small propane grill or a kettle grill, in which case we recommend a steel because a stone will crack from the direct heat under it if used on a regular basis.

TURNING PEEL. This is a must-have if you own a pizza oven. A turning peel has a smaller head that allows you to turn (or rotate) your pizza with ease so you can get an even cook along the crust with just a slight flick of your wrist. If you try to use a larger peel in a smaller oven, it does not turn easily and bumps into the sides of the opening, so buy a pizza turning peel designed to fit your oven.

BOX GRATER. You will use a lot of cheese when making pizza. A good, stable box grater makes life easier. Buying your cheese in bulk saves money, but that means you have to shred it.

MICROPLANE. A Microplane is such an important investment. It can grate garlic for your garlic oil (page 105) or finely grate your Parmigiano-Reggiano or pecorino Romano much more effectively than a box grater.

LARGE METAL SPOON. From applying pizza sauce to evening out your garlic oil drizzle, a large spoon is essential. The backside is the easiest tool to spread out the sauce on your dough.

Nice-to-Have Tools

If you want to go all in, the following make for a better experience.

INSTANT-READ THERMOMETER. This is a different tool than the previously mentioned IR thermometer. For activating yeast, you need warm water: not too hot and not too cold. A good instant-read thermometer is important to assure you have the proper temperature, which for dough is 90 to 105 degrees F. We have used the Thermapen One, an *America's Test Kitchen* favorite, for over a decade.

CLEAR 6-QUART STORAGE CONTAINERS. When done kneading your dough, these containers are great for storing and allowing it to rise. Since they are clear, it's easy to track the rise without moving the dough too much. Be sure to buy the lids if they don't come together. We use the Cambro brand. You can also utilize the same bowls you mixed your dough in, covered with a towel or plastic wrap.

DOUGH PROOFING CONTAINER. Using a rectangular plastic tub with lid, you can store your smaller doughs and allow them to rise together in one bin. It makes for easy storage in your refrigerator or on the counter. Alternatively, you can use sheet pans or baking sheets and cover the dough with plastic wrap.

WOODEN PIZZA PEEL. It's easier to slide pizzas off wooden peels onto your pizza stone. Metal is okay for one pizza, but when you are cranking out multiple pizzas, the hot pizza you just pulled out of the oven is going to leave a metal peel warm and potentially make the next dough stick. Trust us—avoid making calzones by accident and buy a wooden pizza peel. If using a pizza oven, be sure the peel is not wider than the width of its opening.

PERFORATED METAL PIZZA PEEL. Perforated metal peels allow you to shake off any flour from the bottom of the pizza to avoid burning it as you launch your pizza onto the stone or deck. This is especially important for Neapolitan-style pizzas. You need to move fast when using these types of peels; otherwise, you run the risk of some of the dough seeping into the holes and getting stuck, causing the pizza to not slide in. We like to prepare the dough first on a cutting board, then sprinkle the peel with flour (semolina or regular), and build the pizza on it. It's then ready to slide right off while the excess flour falls through the holes, minimizing burning on the base of the pizza.

METAL PIZZA PEEL. When your pizzas are done, it's best to remove them with a metal pizza peel. This allows you to prep the next pizza on the cool wooden peel more effectively. Yes, it's a lot of peels, but trust us: if you launch your pizza from a warm pizza peel, it doesn't slide and you'll end up making a calzone.

CHEF'S TIP: Be sure your pizza peel is not wider than the opening of your pizza oven. Otherwise, you won't be able to slide it in as easily as you need to. Many pizza ovens are 13 inches wide, but check your dimensions first and then purchase the right peel. This is not an issue for grills or your kitchen oven.

PIZZA CUTTER ROCKER. If you want to look like a pizza badass, then grab a pizza cutter rocker that is at least 14 inches large. It's not super practical outside of cutting pizzas, but is very fun to use. Otherwise, you can be practical and use a standard pizza cutter wheel.

STANDARD PIZZA CUTTER. Bigger is better. A large standard cutter is easy to use to cut once through the crust on your cutting board. They have been around for a long time and work. We avoid pizza scissors, which are clunky and not very fun to use or clean. But if you prefer scissors, then by all means go for it!

FOOD PROCESSOR/BLENDER. For your sauces, you'll use an immersion blender or a good quality stand blender. We use the Blendtec blender and it's awesome.

QUART CUPS. Also called deli containers, these are perfect for storing portions of your ingredients in advance, especially if you are planning a pizza party. We use these for our sauces, prepped ingredients, and even individual doughs. They are also a great size for storing frozen dough. You can save and reuse the cups you get from buying takeout, or you can purchase them at a restaurant supply store. Alternatively, you can use any storage containers you already have.

BASTING OR PASTRY BRUSH. A large silicone pastry brush is nice to use when spreading butter or any other fats. It's gentle on the dough and easy to clean.

SERVING TRAYS. Having a set of serving trays that you don't mind cutting pizza on is key. While you can use your cutting boards, if you have more than two pizzas coming off, you'll want dedicated metal trays. The 12-inch trays are great for what we make. Or, if you like larger pizzas, you can get them in 14-inch versions. This practice protects your cutting boards and peels and allows for easy cleaning.

Ingredients

Ingredients matter. Good pizza in the style we are describing here requires few ingredients. Throughout this book we remind you to keep your toppings simple and not overcrowd the dough. Since we're working with so few ingredients, that means using the highest-quality and freshest ones you can find and afford.

FLOUR. As previously mentioned, the flour protein level is critical. We have our favorite flours, like Caputo and King Arthur "00." For the purpose of this book, we wanted to recommend brands you can easily find in your local grocery stores. The exception to this is the Caputo Fioreglut gluten-free flour recommendation, which may need to be ordered online (but it's so worth it).

WATER. We use our local well water for our recipes, but filtered tap water is fine. The key to water in the recipes is making sure it is slightly warmed to activate the yeast properly.

SALT. We use two types of salt throughout our recipes in this cookbook: kosher salt and finishing salt.

- **KOSHER SALT.** Kosher salt (versus iodized table salt) is key when fermenting your doughs. The flavor is richer and more balanced in the mouth. The larger granules were designed for koshering meat and carry through to cooking almost anything. We use Diamond Crystal herein. Not all kosher salts are the same size and weight, so be sure to weigh it.

- **FINISHING SALT.** Finishing salt, like Maldon Sea Salt Flakes or Jacobsen Pure Flake Sea Salt, is a large crystal salt with a high brine taste. It's meant to be sprinkled over finished dishes for a touch of added flavor. We lightly sprinkle finishing salt on every pizza we make, with some exceptions for our dessert pizzas.

YEAST. When making pizza dough, it's best to use active dry yeast in the packets or in bulk. Active yeast requires hydration in warm water to activate it and encourages the two-step fermentation process. That two-step method provides greater complexity in flavor and body for the dough compared to an instant yeast. We do not recommend using instant yeast for pizza dough. It will rise quickly and often overproof, and is best for quick-rise breads.

CHEESE. The types of cheeses you use can elevate a pizza from good to great, familiar to unique, ordinary to outstanding. It's helpful to have a few to choose from that are both hard and soft (higher-hydration) cheeses. Some of our favorites include high-quality Parmigiano-Reggiano, Asiago, fontina, and ricotta, in addition to several balls of fresh mozzarella. Some cheeses won't melt much at all; instead, they will provide a nice texture to a pizza.

Cheese can also add more hydration to a pizza in the instance of wet, fresh mozzarella or ricotta, which can soak in and create a soggy dough. For certain recipes, we'll note whether we recommend using a low-moisture cheese.

CHEESE MATTERS

Always try to select the best quality cheeses you can afford. Since a good pizza doesn't require many ingredients, it's important that quality comes first. Do you sense a theme here? If not, we'll repeat it a few more times. Quality ingredients are important. At right we list a few of our favorites.

CHEESE	TYPE	DESCRIPTION
Asiago	Cow	A pungent and acidic hard cheese that is a great balance to rich, melty cheeses. It's best to use a Microplane to grate the Asiago wedge.
Brie	Cow	Brie is a double-cream cheese with a rind. The rich, almost nutty flavor of the cheese combined with the sharpness of the rind make it a great melty cheese for pizzas. A little goes a long way as Brie has a lot of moisture.
Buffalo Mozzarella (Mozzarella di Bufala)	Italian Buffalo	Made from the milk of Italian Mediterranean buffalo. Although prepped in the same way as fresh mozzarella, buffalo mozzarella is much creamier and a little tangier and acidic. Delicious and expensive.
Cheddar	Cow	Cheddar can have a lot of variation. We typically use sharp yellow cheddar from Tillamook (Oregon coast). It melts well and has a nice, rich flavor with good acidity.
Comté or Gruyère	Cow	A similar style of hard cheese from France and Switzerland, respectively. It's often used for fondue and has great melting capabilities. We like to shred it up to use in cheese dips or as an alternative to Asiago or Brie.
Fresh Mozzarella (Fior di Latte)	Cow	Rich and creamy, often stored in a brine. It's best to drain fresh mozzarella prior to using. We like to shred by hand into similar-sized pieces and place on a paper towel to eliminate excess moisture.
Goat Cheese	Goat	A goat cheese log or chèvre is always in our fridge. Its tangy, pungent flavor is a great balance to richer ingredients.
Low-Moisture Mozzarella	Cow	Unlike the fresh version, low-moisture mozzarella is drier and typically found grated or sliced. It melts well and is great on New York–style pizzas or pizzas we don't want extra moisture on.
Mascarpone	Cow	A sweeter and rich cheese that has the consistency of full-fat yogurt. It still maintains some acidity and is a great base for dessert pizzas.
Parmigiano-Reggiano	Cow	A hard Italian cheese that's salty with lots of flavor. It can take on a rich, nutty flavor profile if aged. You can sub it for Parmesan cheese, but we prefer the taste of this specific regional cheese.
Pecorino Romano	Sheep	A bright and flavorful hard cheese made from sheep's milk. It's a great alternative to Parmigiano-Reggiano if you want a little more acidity and bite.
Ricotta	Cow	Ricotta is all about the texture first and flavor second. Generally, it has a very mild flavor and is great when combined with a hard cheese. We like it because when heated up, it melts slightly but still maintains some texture to it.

OTHER MUST-HAVE INGREDIENTS FOR FINISHING PIZZAS

The finishing touches on a pizza add that special wow factor, elevating it from good to great. We always have some quality finishing salts, oils, and fresh herbs on hand.

- Finishing salt, like Maldon Sea Salt Flakes. Add a pinch to all pizzas when they come out of the oven or grill.
- Good quality extra-virgin olive oil, regular and flavored (like truffle, lemon, or garlic)
- Fresh herbs, like rosemary. We love rosemary on almost any pizza.
- Red pepper flakes
- Hot honey
- Fresh greens, such as arugula or radicchio

Making the Dough and Pizza

After your heat and cooking technique, the flour that becomes the dough is the second most important factor to understand. There is an incredible variety of books that delve deep into the science of pizza dough, like Ken Forkish's *The Elements of Pizza* and *The Pizza Bible* by Tony Gemignani. These authors describe why the dough works the way it does, and if you are a serious pizza person, we recommend both those titles.

Our book isn't meant to be a pizza manifesto or baking encyclopedia, but rather a resource for outdoor pizza cooking. For the sake of getting to our recipes, we want to highlight just a few key points.

FLOUR MATTERS

A great pizza dough starts with good flour. And not all flours are created equal. We aren't talking just about the specific brand, but about the protein content. In order to achieve the texture and level of gluten (a protein found in wheat) that gives great stretch and cooking ability, the right protein levels are key.

You also need to be able to find and afford the flours that work for your particular needs. Many will jump to "00" flour for pizza, a great option highly recommended by many experienced pizzaioli. "00" refers to the grind level and grain size, not the protein content. This type of flour has been very finely milled. When buying flour, the packaging often references a certain range of protein.

The higher the protein levels, the more the gluten strands will connect and create a better texture as the dough ferments and is kneaded. It also allows for more water absorption in the flour. The higher the hydration level, the stickier and denser the flour can become. We knead the dough to help force connection between the proteins. As those connections form and the dough rises, you have the best of both worlds—a strong dough that is difficult to break and will rise further when baking, with a crust that has air pockets and texture you can't wait to bite into.

FLOUR	PROTEIN LEVEL	DESCRIPTION
"00" Flour	10–12 percent	"00" refers to the grind level (think coffee grind levels), not protein content. Various brands have "00" with different protein levels, depending on the strain of wheat.
All-Purpose Flour	8–11 percent	Great in a pinch, but generally makes a less stretchy dough and the flavor profile tends to be more muted.
Bread Flour	12–14 percent	The flour we use almost every time. It's got a high-protein gluten level and tastes very good.
Cake Flour	7–9 percent	This is the lowest level and not recommended for making pizza dough.

NEAPOLITAN PIZZA

Throughout this book we refer often to Neapolitan-style pizzas, and with good reason. Naples, Italy, is the birthplace of modern pizza. It all dates back to seventeenth-century Naples, where pizza was said to have been a street food made with simple ingredients for working-class people. It would take another hundred years to include tomatoes and cheese for pizza to become the worldwide sensation it is today. That wasn't until 1889, when Raffaele Esposito famously created the classic Margherita pizza. Said to have been made for Queen Margherita, he included basil to the cheese and red sauce to honor the colors of the Italian flag and presented it to the queen when she was visiting the region, expanding the style of flatbreads that were already being made in Naples. Needless to say it was a hit, a food fit for a queen, and hence the pizza named after this event is one used at almost all quality pizzerias worldwide.

Not long after that, Italian immigrants brought this style to North America, introducing it to New York and creating new styles of this beloved dish, which eventually spread to the rest of the country and world. Now, pizza is no longer just a simple street food, it's a lifestyle.

Neapolitan is such an important style of pizza that it's been given a protected designation within Italy that is generally respected throughout the world and managed by the international nonprofit organization Associazione Verace Pizza Napoletana (AVPN).

Unlike Champagne (a protected name), sparkling wines produced from grapes found exclusively in the Champagne region of France, a Neapolitan pizza (also a protected name) can be made anywhere in the world so long as it respects the origins and very specific requirements set by the AVPN.

Those requirements include, but are not limited to, the style of tomatoes and where they come from for the sauce, the type of buffalo mozzarella used and where it originates (Campania), and the specific wheat and type of yeast for the flour (no sugar, no fats like oil). The rules also mention cooking methods and the precise time it takes to cook a pizza (between 60 and 90 seconds). Anyone can be trained in making this style of pizza, with a focus not just on the technique but on the history of the pizza form. We deeply respect the history of this pizza style and the work involved in maintaining its authenticity all over the world.

Throughout this book, we reference Neapolitan-style pizza (or Neapolitan-inspired pizza), which is not the same as a true, authentic Neapolitan pizza. We do this to honor the designation and the style while acknowledging that not everyone can source the exact Italian tomatoes or find the specific cheeses allowed. It also offers you the flexibility to be able to create something different. Our goal is to get as close as we can to the real thing, while using the ingredients, tools, and techniques available to us. For any pizza lover interested in the true art of Neapolitan pizza, we encourage you to visit the AVPN website and consider taking one of its training classes offered online or in person throughout the world.

Stay away from self-rising flours; they won't give you the desired texture and rise since a leavening agent and salt are already added to the flour.

We generally use bread flour, which provides a nice balance in protein and gluten content. Occasionally we will blend 20 percent "00" flour with bread flour, which reduces the protein levels. When we use "00" flour, we use Caputo or King Arthur.

HYDRATION LEVELS

We are now entering full nerd territory, but there's a very important process to making good dough, especially when you are matching the right dough to your style of grill or pizza oven.

That is the ratio of water to flour, also known as the hydration level, or baker's percentage. It's often referred to by pizza nerds like us as a percentage. If you hear the question, "What hydration level was your dough?" you take the total amount of water divided by the total amount of flour. So a 67 percent hydration dough contains 325 grams of water and 500 grams of flour. You can now speak pizza code. You're welcome.

Hydration affects not only how much dough you make (the higher hydration, the more yield) but also the texture of the crust and how long the dough takes to cook. The higher the hydration level, the denser the dough will become. If you overhydrate a low-protein dough, it gets too sticky. If you underhydrate a high-protein dough, it will be very dry and difficult to work with.

For this book, we use the following hydration levels based on the dough we recommend for your grill or pizza oven.

- **NEAPOLITAN-STYLE DOUGH:** 67 percent hydration using bread flour—perfect for dedicated pizza ovens.
- **NEW YORK-STYLE DOUGH:** 70 percent hydration using bread flour—perfect for any grill that isn't a pizza oven.
- **GLUTEN-FREE DOUGH:** 80 percent hydration level using gluten-free flour—perfect for a grill or pizza oven.

For grilled pizzas, it's especially important to note that the lower your heat gets, the more you want hydration in your dough so the pizza doesn't burn. Dough that has more hydration takes longer to cook as the water evaporates, and grilling pizzas takes longer than cooking in a dedicated pizza oven. Making sense?

- Have a Big Green Egg or kettle grill that tops out at 600 degrees F? Consider using a 70–75 percent hydration dough.
- Using an Ooni or Gozney pizza oven at 900 degrees F? Then consider a 60–67 percent hydration level.

This ratio is also an important part of knowing how to scale up your recipe. Just keep the ratios and modestly adjust the salt and yeast levels proportionately.

This is why we strongly encourage you to buy a good digital scale, because it's going to be your friend for making perfectly proportioned dough. It will also allow you to easily adjust how many doughs you want to make. Our recipes will yield three doughs. So if you want to make a single dough, understanding the ratios will help you adjust to any number of doughs you wish to make.

CHEF'S TIP: If you don't have one yet, stop what you're doing and get yourself a good quality digital kitchen scale immediately. Consider it an investment in your pizza game and a gift to yourself! We use the Escali digital scale.

LEAVENING

After choosing the flour, the next important thing is understanding the fermentation process. The best pizza dough recipes allow time for the yeast to activate, feed, and expand the dough. Combined with kneading and forming the gluten strands, the important process of leavening shouldn't be rushed.

Active dry yeast is best; you add it to lukewarm water so it has the ideal temperature to "wake up" and start the feeding process. If the water is too hot, it will kill the yeast. If it's too cool, it dramatically slows the fermentation process. We recommend the water be warmed between 90 and 110 degrees F (32 and 43 degrees C).

FIRST RISE. Also referred to as the bulk rise, or fermentation. The first rise is like waking up the yeast and introducing it to the party in the flour. It starts as you feed the yeast with warm water and combine it with the dry ingredients. It expands the dough as the yeast feeds.

SECOND RISE. While you can technically roll out the first-rise dough into dough balls, adding a second fermentation period allows the yeast to continue to feed while you connect those gluten strands for great dough texture as you knead the dough. The second rise is when you've formed the individual dough balls from the first rise.

We recommend you plan for both the bulk fermentation and the secondary proofing of your dough; don't skip this step! Ideally plan a minimum of 5 hours at room temperature (at least 70 degrees F, or 21 degrees C) to get the right amount of rise and texture.

WHY KNEAD? As we mentioned, by pressing, folding, and pushing on your dough, you are forcing the proteins to combine and create an intricate highway of gluten strands. If you were to pull apart a well-kneaded dough, you would see strands that look like spiderwebs, so it's key to make sure you knead. The exception is when working with gluten-free dough, which is an entirely different beast (more on that later).

If making a same-day dough, the dough will rise if the ambient temperature of your home is between 70 and 80 degrees F (21 and 26 degrees C). If it's cooler than that, a great hack is to turn on just the light in your oven. Then place your fermenting dough in the oven while the light is on, which will keep the dough just warm enough. If your home is cooler, it takes longer for the rising to happen.

If your home is hotter, then you may run the risk of overproofing. If your home temperature is over 80 degrees F, monitor your dough to see if it's expanding too fast after the second rise. If that is happening,

knead the dough balls again to tighten them up after the second fermentation. Just don't do this less than 60 minutes prior to making pizza, as the dough balls need to settle to have those important air pockets.

If you are letting your dough rise in the refrigerator for 24–48 hours, then make the dough through the first fermentation process as noted. When you break down the larger dough balls into individual-sized balls, roll them tight and pinch them to create a solid dough. Then place in a dough proofing container or on a sheet tray covered with plastic wrap.

Cold fermentation in the refrigerator has a few benefits. First, it slows down the proofing process, which minimizes overproofing or the formation of huge bubbles. Second, it allows more time for the yeast to work its magic, leading to a more airy crust with more flavor.

Our recommendation is to give your dough 24 hours: 2 hours for the bulk fermentation at room temperature and then secondary proofing as dough balls in the refrigerator. Then remove from the refrigerator 2 hours before using so they aren't too cold to work with when forming the pizza rounds. But if you do wake up wanting dough that same day, give yourself a minimum of 5 hours.

PRE-FERMENTATION STARTERS: BIGA, POOLISH, AND SOURDOUGH

Using pre-fermented starters is a common way to increase the flavor and texture of your pizza dough, although it is not required. These styles of starters are pre-fermented mixes that you add (in portions) to your dough ingredients. The fermentation that has already started from the pre-ferment carries over to your pizza dough.

SALT AND YEAST

There are some who adamantly say that adding salt to your warm water as the yeast wakes up actually kills or inhibits the yeast. It won't kill the yeast, but salt *will* slow down the fermentation process. So we like to balance that by adding our salt to the flour and then mixing with the water and yeast mixture.

- **BIGA**. Biga is a traditional dough starter that is more solid in texture and uses commercial yeast.
- **POOLISH**. Poolish doughs have a pre-fermentation base, with a more glue- or paste-like texture. Poolish starters use commercial yeasts.
- **SOURDOUGH**. Sourdough is a pre-fermentation starter that uses the natural yeasts in the environment instead of commercial yeast; it's more paste-like in texture.

For this book, we keep things simple and do not use these types of starters. They take longer to proof and more advance planning, but we encourage you to visit our website to experiment with various pre-fermentation starters.

PREPARING THE PIZZA

Your dough is made, fermentation is done, and now it's time to shape the dough and make your perfect pizza. There are a few more important steps we need to walk through.

The ideal dough to form into pizza is just below room temperature (65–68 degrees F or 18–20 degrees C). So if you did a longer fermentation in the refrigerator, take it out 2 hours before you plan to make pizzas. If you waited too long, turn on the light in your oven and let it warm up there, covered, for up to an hour.

The key is that the dough is room temperature, soft (but not too soft), and ready to work with. If it's still cold, it won't stretch. If it's too warm (overproofed), then you have to re-form it, which will minimize those air pockets or potentially rip it while forming your pizza round.

FORMING PIZZA DOUGH

It's time to set up your workspace.

We like to work on a large surface, like a big wooden cutting board, marble or granite slab, or even a clean countertop. The key is to have a large, organized workspace to do your thing. It will help you get in the zone and keep things structured to create some beautiful pizzas. We use a large enough space to shape our doughs and have all ingredients nearby and accessible, laid out like an assembly line. Give yourself at least 2 to 3 feet of surface area to work with, including your ingredients prepped and ready to go. You want your surface to be dry. We like to have 1 cup of bread flour and 1 cup of semolina flour right in front of us for dusting.

Have a bowl with your sauces on one side, the cheeses ready in the middle, and the toppings in separate bowls or containers on the other side. Place the ingredients in layering order.

Each type of dough will have a different method of shaping. For the dough recipes in this book, we form them by hand, no rolling pin needed!

For a traditional Neapolitan dough, there is a classic stretch-and-slap method used by pizzaioli that works your forearms. It's a very fast and useful method, but when we've taught pizza classes to groups of beginners, we tend to see fear in students' eyes, as if we're asking them to perform magic.

For the beginners, we've found an easier way to get started that's much less intimidating than the fast-paced stretch-and-slap, but still yields great results. Then, after you've mastered forming your dough into an identifiable circular shape, you can venture to YouTube to watch how the masters do it.

The idea is to create some thickness on the rim for the crust, but not too much, and to have a thinner base for the ingredients. We've learned that people have different opinions on how much thickness to leave. We like a medium amount, but have seen some pizza makers create very thick rims, while others leave very little. Once you get the fundamentals down, you'll find and lean into your own personal preference. Our method here will result in a mild rise to the crust.

Once you have your space set up (your mise en place), lightly flour your work surface with bread flour. Place the dough on the floured surface. We do not recommend the use of coarse cornmeal or another coarse grain, which will impart an unpleasant crunch and texture when cooking. Regular flour is all you need.

Using your fingers, start gently pressing from the center of the dough and pushing toward the outer rim, leaving about ½ inch of the rim untouched, continually working the dough from the center to the outside. Push the excess air toward the rim carefully, without touching the rim, leaving thickness on the edge. Then flip the dough, rotate it, and repeat, slowly rotating the dough so it maintains an even thickness.

When it's 6 or 7 inches in diameter, gently pick up the dough with both hands so that it hangs down vertically. Start rotating and stretching the dough, slightly pulling (almost pinching) the rim (without damaging the edge) and rotating through the entire circumference of the dough, until it looks even. You may need to do a couple of rotations until it's smooth and level.

Then use your knuckles under the dough and very gently pull it, with your knuckles tucked near the rim edges. Gently pull the knuckles away from each other, until you reach your desired circumference, which is 11–12 inches for the Neapolitan-style pizza doughs and 12–13 inches for New York-style.

Your dough is now ready to place on your pizza peel. Dust your pizza peel with semolina flour (or bread flour if you don't have semolina) and then place the dough on the peel. We like to shake the peel to make sure the dough slides back and forth so it will launch easily into the pizza oven or onto the pizza stone. Now start adding your toppings.

If you encounter a tear, don't freak out and start over. Just give it a pinch to close the hole, and that should do the trick. Just don't stretch your dough too thin; otherwise, it won't be able to hold your toppings. Aim for no more than 11–12 inches, and you'll be fine!

This method works for both dough styles in this book (Neapolitan and New York). For the Gluten-Free Dough, there will be a separate method mentioned in that recipe.

CHEF'S TIP: DO NOT USE A ROLLING PIN when forming dough. No, we're not shouting. If you use a rolling pin, you will destroy all those amazing air pockets you took painstaking time to develop in the rise process, so it's important to use your hands. Also, use semolina or bread flour instead of cornmeal to dust your peel. When cooking pizza, the cornmeal will add a crunchy texture and will burn, especially on a really hot pizza deck. If you are nervous about the pizza sliding off your peel, be sure you are not overloading your pizza, have a good smooth peel, and have lots of flour under the dough.

BUILDING A PIZZA

Once your dough is formed, you'll want to work fast when building your pizza to get it on the oven or grill successfully without any casualties. These doughs are delicate, so once you shape the dough, top them soon after and immediately transfer to the oven or grill.

The key here is to not overload the pizza! This was hard for Mary to accept, since she wants to put everything on a pizza. Small quantities are integral to pizza success.

Repeat: don't overload your pizza.

Okay, now let's make a pizza.

Start by spreading a small amount of sauce (be it tomato sauce, white sauce, pesto, you name it). A little goes a long way. For a Neapolitan style, our rough go-to is around ¼ cup to ⅓ cup of sauce. Make sure to leave the rim free of sauce. Our preference is to spread the sauce to about ½ inch from the rim for a moderate crust (but you might like more of a thick crust). The backside of a large spoon is the perfect utensil to even out the sauce.

Now, evenly spread out your toppings. The goal is twofold: to not add so much weight to the dough that it won't slide off the peel smoothly and to maintain the integrity of its shape.

Next, give your peel a quick little shimmy shake to make sure the pizza will slide. If it doesn't, don't freak out. Just figure out where the dough is too wet (or sticky), then gently lift that side of the dough a couple of inches off the peel and toss some semolina flour under that area. Then test again to see if it will slide. Keep dusting more flour under the dough until you can feel the whole pizza shake. It's now ready to load into your oven or onto your grill of choice.

Immediately transfer your pizza to your pizza oven; the longer the loaded pizza sits on your peel, the harder it will be to slide into your oven. Do this quickly and with confidence. Channel your inner pizza master and don't overthink it. The process of sliding your dough from the peel into the oven can be a little scary the first couple of times you do it. This is why we always start our pizza nights with an easy pizza, like a margherita, or something with very little to no toppings. Once you get the hang of the toss, you'll be able to sling pizza like a master! It just takes a few times to get used to the process.

Cook the pizza according to the oven of choice. Dedicated pizza ovens have different cooking methods and times from those of a grill.

And remember, don't overload your pizza. You'll thank us later.

TROUBLESHOOTING YOUR PIZZA

What do I do if my dough seems too wet?

Not all flour brands are the same, and while baker's percentages generally work, you can have an instance where your dough is too wet. If that is the case, dust a generous amount of flour on your working surface. Knead the dough to incorporate the flour until it reaches the desired consistency.

What if my dough is too dry and hard to work with?

If your dough is too difficult to knead because it's dry, add small amounts of water to the top of the dough as you work it until it reaches the desired consistency.

My dough isn't rising in the first proof.

First, make sure your ambient temperature is warm enough to encourage the rise. Use the oven trick by turning the light on in your oven if the temp of your house is under 70 degrees F (21 degrees C). The oven light will typically keep the oven warm to around 75 degrees F (24 degrees C).

The second common reason for lack of rise is that your yeast is dead. As you activate the yeast in warm water, you should see some small bubbles or foaming as it's warmed and waking up. If you don't, it may not rise. It's best to start over.

What do I do if my dough is overproofed?

Overproofing is evident when your pizza dough swells and has oversized air pockets in it. It's most common if you used too much yeast or it's too warm when proofing, or if you're using leftover dough from a pizza night. The easy fix for overproofing is to knead the dough, re-form it into a dough ball, and allow the dough ball to rise again for another 2 hours.

What do I do if my dough has dried out and is cracking just prior to making pizza?

To prevent this, be sure you are proofing your dough in a proofing container or wrapped in plastic wrap on a sheet tray. But if your dough looks dry on top with some slight cracking or spots, get a paper towel wet with water and wring it out so that it's not dripping wet. Place the damp towel over the dough and cover with plastic wrap. This will rehydrate the outer portion of the dough, making it easier to work with.

My dough tore while I was forming my pizza round.
It's okay if the dough breaks while you are shaping it. You can pinch the dough back together with your fingers.

My pizza crust is too thick after baking.
As your pizza bakes, the crust will rise, and you want that. But too much rising leads to a really doughy crust. This is an indication that you didn't stretch out the dough enough. So for the next pizza, increase the width and press out the dough edges. We generally allow a ½-inch crust before cooking.

My toppings aren't cooking in my pizza oven.
Be sure your stone and grill or oven are at the correct temperature. If you find that some of your toppings aren't cooking to your desired texture, especially on a pizza oven, then consider cooking the toppings in advance. This is especially important for mushrooms and onions, which have a higher water content. We also do not recommend making any pizza with raw meat, with the exception of the deep dish; you want it to reach the proper internal temperature, so cook it in advance to be safe.

My crust is burning before my toppings are done.
This is indicative of a pizza stone that is too hot. We always have two pizza stones, and if one gets too hot, we swap it out for a new one and allow it to warm up. Another option to cool it down is to lower the temperature of your grill or pizza oven. This will take some additional time, but eventually it will cool. That is why we opt to have two pizza stones.

Another option is to place a cast-iron pan on the stone, reducing some of the heat. The stone will release some of its heat onto the cast-iron pan. When you remove the pan, the surface of the pizza stone should have cooled enough.

RECIPES

DELIGHTFUL DOUGHS AND SAUCES

The goal of this book is to empower you to mix and match dough, sauce, and toppings to create your own amazing pizzas. But we have included some of our classic pizza recipes that we enjoy almost weekly with our kids and friends. Whether a breakfast-inspired pizza or a sweet dessert pizza, these are sure to inspire you (and taste amazing).

Choosing the Right Dough for Your Grill or Oven

For grilled pizzas, the dough should match your style of cooker for best results. As your temperatures increase for your pizza stone, the more you can move to a lower-hydration dough, like Neapolitan-style.

PIZZA STONE TEMPERATURE	DESCRIPTION
Under 500 degrees F	New York–Style Deep-Dish
Between 500 and 700 degrees F	New York–Style Deep-Dish Neapolitan–Style
Over 700 degrees F	Neapolitan–Style

Our Gluten-Free Dough can be used at all heat levels.

FREEZING DOUGH

If you have leftover dough or you want to plan ahead, you can freeze any of our doughs for up to 3 months. After the second proof, wrap the dough ball tightly in plastic wrap and freeze.

If you are freezing leftover dough that has already been sitting out, re-form it into a tight dough ball. Wrap in plastic wrap and freeze.

To thaw, take the dough ball out of the freezer the day before making pizza and place it in the refrigerator to slowly thaw. Then remove the dough ball from the refrigerator 2 hours prior to using to bring to room temperature. We like to remove the plastic wrap and place the dough on a sheet tray dusted with flour or lined with parchment paper. We then cover the sheet tray with plastic wrap so the dough doesn't dry out.

MAKING PIZZA DOUGH

1

2

3

4

5

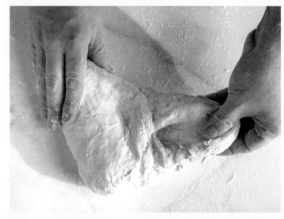

6

7

8

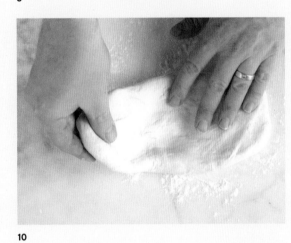

9

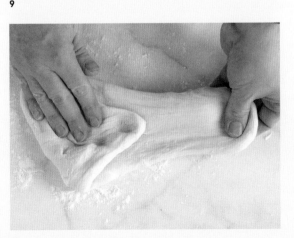

10

11

12

**YIELD: 3 (260–285 G)
DOUGH BALLS**

335 g warm water (95–105
degrees F)—67 percent
hydration dough
½ teaspoon active dry yeast
(just shy of 1 g)
500 g bread flour (or
"00" if you want the
authentic version)
12 g kosher salt
Extra-virgin olive oil,
for greasing

NEAPOLITAN-STYLE DOUGH

Neapolitan pizza, or pizza Napoletana, is a specific pizza that originated in Naples, Italy, and is now governed by the True Neapolitan Pizza Association (Associazione Verace Pizza Napoletana, or AVPN). The AVPN regulations maintain authenticity of both the dough and the pizzas that are inspired by the region as well as protect the heritage of the pizza's origin. When it comes to grilling, we do take some liberty based on the availability of ingredients for the general public.

Neapolitan dough contains four ingredients: flour, water, salt, and yeast. The flour is supposed to be a "00" or "0" milled flour. However, we use bread flour, which is more readily available and more affordable. There is no sugar or oil in this style of dough, as you would see in a New York–style pizza dough, which was inspired by the Neapolitan dough.

This dough is perfect for high-heat outdoor pizza ovens that can maintain a 900-degree F oven with a 700-degree F pizza stone. The texture of the pizza is a soft dough with a crust that rises with air pockets formed from the fermentation.

- In a large bowl, add the warm water and yeast. Stir to combine and then let sit for 5 minutes. The warm water will start to activate the yeast.

- In another large bowl, combine the flour and salt.

- Add the flour mixture to the bowl of water and combine with your hands for 30 seconds. Incorporate the dry flour from the edges.

- In the bowl, roughly form the dough into a ball, then cover with plastic wrap or a thick towel. Let it rise for 20 minutes. After 20 minutes, the yeast has activated, the dough is starting to rise, and it's time for the first fermentation.

- Lightly flour your hands and a cutting board, then gently remove the dough from the bowl and place on the board. Knead the dough for 30 seconds by gently folding the dough like a trifold wallet and pressing down firmly with the palms of your hands. We do this about four times (over the course of 30 seconds). Begin to form the dough ball by cupping it with your hands. The seam from folding is on the bottom, and the top should be smooth. Place the dough ball into a lightly oiled (we use olive oil) bowl, seam side down, cover with plastic wrap, and let it rise somewhere warm for 2 hours.

- After 2 hours, the dough will have risen and it's time to separate it into individual balls. We typically weigh it and divide by 3 for 11- to 12-inch pizzas. Using a pizza scraper, divide the dough into 250–280 g balls. After dividing the dough, knead the smaller dough balls again for 30 seconds and re-form into balls. Place them on a floured sheet pan and flour the tops (so they don't stick). Cover tightly with plastic wrap.

- Let the dough balls rise in a warm spot for 4–6 additional hours. Then they are ready to use for your favorite pizza recipes.

- If you are making dough the day prior for a 24-hour rise, follow the same instructions. After the first rise is done and the smaller dough balls are formed, dust the tops with flour. Cover them tightly with plastic wrap and then place in the refrigerator. Don't crowd the dough balls or they will rise into each other. Remove from the refrigerator 2 hours before you plan to bake them so they can come to room temperature.

HYDRATION LEVELS

One important aspect of pizza dough is understanding hydration levels, or baker's percentage. This is the ratio of water to flour in any given recipe. If you see recipes that call for an 80% hydration, that means that the water weight is 80 percent of the weight of the flour. So if you have 1,000 grams of flour, then you add 800 grams of (warm) water to the mix.

Hydration levels can be adjusted based on preference. Once you know your preferred percentages for each dough, you can easily scale up or down based on the percentage. We recommend you start with the hydration levels in the recipes, then adjust based on your preference and setting (some environments will need more or less, based on where you live and the climate).

YIELD: 3 (260–310 G) DOUGH BALLS

350 g warm water (95–105 degrees F)—70 percent hydration dough

3 tablespoons extra-virgin olive oil, plus more for greasing

½ teaspoon active dry yeast

500 g bread flour (or "00" if you want the authentic version)

15 g cane sugar

12 g kosher salt

ALL-PURPOSE NEW YORK– INSPIRED DOUGH

New York–inspired doughs were created by Italian immigrants wanting the Neapolitan-style flavor and texture but having access to different styles of ovens at lower heat. The main difference is the addition of olive oil and sugar, as well as higher-hydration level, which makes for a dough that has more stretch to it and is cooked at a lower temperature.

We use a New York–style dough if we cook on any grill that isn't a dedicated high-heat pizza oven or if we plan a lower-heat recipe. An example is our bread sticks.

When using a grill or your home oven, the pizza stone will likely cap at 575 degrees F. Any higher and the grill may run the risk of being damaged.

- In a large bowl, add the warm water, olive oil, and yeast. Stir to combine and then let sit for 5 minutes. The warm water will start to activate the yeast.

- In another large bowl, combine the flour, sugar, and salt.

- Add the flour mixture to the bowl of water and combine with your hands for 30 seconds. Incorporate the dry flour from the edges.

- In the bowl, roughly form the dough into a ball, then cover with plastic wrap or a thick towel. Let it rise for 20 minutes. After 20 minutes, the yeast has activated, the dough is starting to rise, and it's time to knead for the first fermentation.

- Lightly flour your hands and a cutting board, then gently remove the dough from the bowl and place on the board. Knead the dough for 30 seconds by gently folding the dough like a trifold wallet and pressing down firmly with the palms of your hands. We do this about four times (over the course of 30 seconds). Begin to form the dough into a ball by cupping it with your hands. The seam from folding is on the bottom, and the top should be smooth. Place the dough ball into a lightly oiled (we use olive oil) bowl, seam side down, cover with plastic wrap, and let it rise in the ambient temperature of 72–80 degrees F for 2 hours.

- After 2 hours, the dough will have risen and it's time to separate it into individual balls. We typically weigh it and divide by 3 for 11- to 12-inch pizzas. Using a pizza scraper, divide the dough into 260–310 g balls. After dividing the dough, knead the smaller dough balls again for 30 seconds and re-form into balls. Place them on a floured sheet pan and flour the tops (so they don't stick). Cover tightly with plastic wrap.

- Let the dough balls rise somewhere warm for 4–6 additional hours. Then they are ready to use for your favorite pizza recipes.

- If you are making the day prior for a 24-hour rise, follow the same instructions. After the first rise is done and the smaller dough balls are formed, dust the tops with flour. Cover them tightly with plastic wrap and then place in the refrigerator. Don't crowd the dough balls or they will rise into each other. Remove from the refrigerator 2 hours before you plan to make them so they can come to room temperature.

400 g warm water
1 package active dry yeast
500 g gluten-free flour
   (we highly recommend
   Caputo Fioreglut)
12 g kosher salt
12 g baking powder
Extra-virgin olive oil, for
   greasing

GLUTEN-FREE DOUGH

We have tried almost every major cup-for-cup gluten-free flour in our search for a good GF pizza dough option. Having a solid gluten-free pizza dough recipe in your toolbox is important, given how many people aren't eating gluten these days. And our kids have been gluten-free for years. We don't want to deprive them of the magic of a great pizza, so after fumbling with creating our own mix—which contained lots of different hard-to-find flours—we decided it was best to find a premade mix that actually worked.

Each brand has a unique blend of flours and starches that changes the nature of each flour when water is added. For our Gluten-Free Dough we use Caputo Fioreglut, which is available at finer grocery stores or online and uses an 80% hydration.

It's so good that many people can't tell the difference from other flours. It's a little pricey, but we promise it's worth it! If you use other gluten-free flours, start with a 70% hydration first so the dough is not too wet. If you need to add more water, add as needed.

- In a large bowl, add the warm water and then the yeast. Stir to combine and let sit for 5 minutes.

- In another bowl, combine the flour, salt, and baking powder.

- After 5 minutes, slowly add the flour mixture into the water and combine with your hands. The dough will be slightly sticky. Incorporate with your hands until the dough is formed into a rough ball.

- Place a handful of the gluten-free flour on a large cutting board. Carefully remove the pizza dough and knead it for 30 seconds to form one ball. Use the palms of your hands to press on the dough, then fold it in half and press again. Do this four times and, cupping your hands, form into a dough ball.

- Place the dough into a lightly oiled container (we use olive oil) and cover. Allow to ferment for 2 hours. The dough ball will start to rise.

- After 2 hours, remove the dough from the container and weigh it. Divide the number on the scale by 3 and shape into three equal dough balls. Form with your hands in a manner similar to earlier kneading.

- Place the pizza dough on a sheet tray or in a dough proofing container. Lightly flour the top of the balls and cover with plastic wrap or container lid. Let sit for 3 hours for the second fermentation. The dough will rise again.

- After the second fermentation, the dough balls are ready to make into pizzas.

A NOTE ON THE GLUTEN-FREE DOUGH: When working with this dough, it will feel almost like Play-Doh compared to what you'd expect from a gluten dough. That's normal. You won't be able to shape this dough in the same way as balls made from gluten.

Keep thinking about this like Play-Doh. Start with a circular dough disk or ball, and press it out into a circular shape. We still don't use a rolling pin, because you will flatten the outside rim (and these pizzas can still make beautiful rims if you don't flatten them first). Gently press the inside toward the outside, leaving ½ inch of the rim untouched. If it's hard to work with, grab a small glass and use that in place of a rolling pin to smooth out the center to get it to that 11-inch round you're aiming for, again avoiding the rim.

Just keep pressing or using a small glass to smooth out the center until you get to the desired circumference. The rim may crack a bit. That's okay. Just like Play-Doh, re-form the rim using your fingers, trying not to flatten it. Once you get there, dust more GF flour under the dough, and build your pizza. The same rule applies for these pizzas: don't overcrowd your pizza with toppings.

4 tablespoons softened
   unsalted butter
3 garlic cloves,
   very finely minced
¼ teaspoon kosher salt

MAGIC GARLIC BUTTER

This garlic butter is perfect as a base to any flatbread or pizza with a white sauce. There's really nothing "magic" to making it, but it adds amazing flavor dimensions. For ease, you can make a larger batch, then roll it into a log in plastic wrap and store in the refrigerator for months. Remove a few tablespoons at a time as you need it. It's best if the garlic butter is softened or comes to room temperature before using; otherwise, it won't spread onto the dough properly.

- In a small bowl, combine the butter, garlic, and salt. Stir with a fork to combine.

- Brush onto pizza dough before adding any sauces or toppings.

NOTE: We like to use a garlic press for finer consistency versus dicing. Or use a Microplane to get an even finer garlic texture.

GARLIC OIL

Garlic oil may seem like such a basic ingredient, but it adds the little extra flavor that takes many of our pizzas from good to great. This is not infused olive oil; it's a quick oil flavor that we make the day we are going to use it. We do not recommend making this too far in advance because it's not technically a pasteurized infused oil. You can also substitute a store-bought infused garlic oil and then add salt for flavor.

- In a small bowl, combine the olive oil and salt.

- With a Microplane, grate the garlic into the bowl. Stir to combine.

- Use within 24 hours.

SCALING UP: Double or triple the recipe as needed if you plan to bake more than two pizzas.

YIELD: ¼ CUP, ENOUGH FOR TWO PIZZAS

¼ cup olive oil
⅛ teaspoon kosher salt
1 large garlic clove, peeled

1 (28-ounce) can San
   Marzano whole peeled
   tomatoes, strained of
   excess liquid
½ teaspoon kosher salt

NEAPOLITAN-INSPIRED RED SAUCE

The classic Neapolitan-inspired red sauce is only two ingredients—quality canned tomatoes and kosher salt—and requires no cooking. The most important thing to know when making this style of sauce is to buy the best quality tomatoes you can find. We only use San Marzano whole peeled tomatoes (ideally from Italy), which are rich, thick, and naturally sweet. This can be made the day before. You can also use a food mill, blender, or food processor, but we love doing this by hand. It's a great way to release pent-up stress.

- Crush the whole tomatoes with your hands in a large bowl. Add the salt and stir to combine.

CHEF'S TIP: Not all canned tomatoes are the same. Some are in thicker puree, and some are in liquid that is thinner. For the ones in liquid, drain some of the excess prior to mixing. If you don't drain the excess liquid, the sauce will be too runny. You can save the excess to use later for soup. Salt to taste starting with our portions. The more volume the more salt needed. Jazz up the flavor by adding some fresh chopped basil leaves.

CLASSIC RED SAUCE

This no-cook all-purpose red sauce is like the New York–style pizza sauces many of us grew up with. It's a balance of good tomatoes, lots of herbs and seasonings, and the right level of acidity. It's best to make this sauce in advance to allow the flavors to integrate.

- In a food processor, grind the dry ingredients. This breaks up the fennel so you don't get big chunks. Add the tomatoes, tomato paste, olive oil, and honey and pulse to combine.

- Taste and adjust flavors as desired.

YIELD: 2 CUPS

½ teaspoon dried oregano

½ teaspoon dried basil

¼ teaspoon dried
  fennel seed

¼ teaspoon garlic powder

¼ teaspoon kosher salt

¼ teaspoon red
  pepper flakes

1 (15-ounce) can whole
  peeled tomatoes, drained
  of excess liquid

1 tablespoon tomato paste

½ teaspoon extra-virgin
  olive oil

½ teaspoon honey

Marinara

To create a thicker base for the pizza sauce, dipping sauce for breadsticks, and the deep dish pizza, we like to use tomato paste. This will create a deeper flavor in the classic sauce. Feel free to add more tomato paste if you like a really rich sauce.

- To make the Marinara: mix 1 cup of the Classic Red Sauce with 2 tablespoons tomato paste.

YIELD: 1 CUP

1 tablespoon unsalted
  butter
1 tablespoon all-purpose
  flour (can substitute
  gluten-free flour)
1 cup whole milk
1 teaspoon chopped
  fresh rosemary
½ teaspoon kosher salt

BASIC WHITE SAUCE

A béchamel is the classic "white sauce" you will find in many pizza restaurants. You can add more flavor or cheese to this recipe to give it more of an alfredo taste, but the goal of this sauce is a creamy, rich texture that lets the toppings really shine, so we keep this basic. This portion is good for up to four smaller pizzas or two large pizzas.

- In a small saucepan over medium heat, melt the butter.

- Add the flour and whisk to make a roux. After 3 minutes of stirring, the mixture should be bubbling and golden in color.

- Add the milk, rosemary, and salt and continue to whisk as the mixture combines and comes to a simmer. Continue to whisk and allow to simmer and thicken for an additional 10 minutes. Do not let it boil; if needed, lower the heat to keep a simmer.

- Remove from the heat and let cool. Can be made up to 2 days in advance if stored in the refrigerator.

HAZELNUT PESTO

YIELD: JUST OVER 2 CUPS

2 cups fresh basil
½ cup toasted hazelnuts
½ cup freshly grated
   Parmigiano-Reggiano
½ cup good extra-virgin
   olive oil
2 garlic cloves
1 tablespoon lemon juice
1 teaspoon kosher salt
1 teaspoon coarse
   black pepper

This recipe is a nod to our Oregon home, the hazelnut capital of the United States. Hazelnuts make for a delicious alternative to a pine nut pesto, and offer the perfect base for any pizza calling for a pesto sauce. If you like an oilier pesto, feel free to add more olive oil (about 1 tablespoon at a time).

- In a food processor, add the basil, hazelnuts, cheese, olive oil, garlic, lemon juice, salt, and pepper. Pulse until combined. Texture should be fine and not too liquid.

- Will last up to a month in the refrigerator before it starts to oxidize.

1 cup honey
2 tablespoons apple
  cider vinegar
2 tablespoons red
  pepper flakes

CLASSIC HOT HONEY

Hot honey has become a wild trend throughout the country, now available everywhere from grocery stores to restaurants. The sweet honey combined with savory and heat elements make for a delicious condiment that we use on everything from honey butter to a charcuterie board to a pizza drizzle. The spicy flavors are very mild and add an excellent finishing touch to many of the pizza recipes in this book. It's a condiment that we now always keep stocked in our pantry.

- In a small saucepan over medium heat, combine the honey, apple cider vinegar, and red pepper flakes. Bring to a simmer, then reduce the heat and stir.

- Continue to simmer on low heat for 20 minutes to let the chili pepper flavor infuse. The honey will liquefy, which is normal. Keep the heat as low as you can to maintain a simmer; if the honey is bubbling over, the heat is too high.

- Remove from the heat and place in a container (we like a glass mason jar). The honey will thicken as it cools and will last up to 3 months in a dark cupboard. Optional: You can strain it if desired, but it's not necessary.

EASY CHIMICHURRI

YIELD: 1 CUP

Chimichurri is most often associated as a condiment for beef, popular in South American cooking. But to us, chimichurri is our all-the-things-topping for anything from grilled meats to salad dressings, to using as a finishing sauce. It also makes for a great base for a pizza, especially one that has grilled meat as the star. The flavor is bright, acidic, and heats well on a pizza.

- Place parsley, garlic, shallot, vinegar, lemon juice, fresh oregano, salt, pepper, and red pepper flakes in the food processor. Pulse a few times until everything starts to break up.

- Start slowly adding the olive oil. Start with just ½ cup, then slowly add more and pulse a few times. Don't puree, just a few pulses will do. If it's too thick add more olive oil until you get to your desired consistency.

2 cups fresh Italian parsley, loosely packed

5 garlic cloves, peeled and smashed

2 tablespoons roughly chopped shallots

2 tablespoons red wine vinegar

½ lemon, juiced (about 2 tablespoons)

1 tablespoon chopped fresh oregano

1 teaspoon salt

½ teaspoon pepper

½ teaspoon red pepper flakes

½ to ¾ cup extra-virgin olive oil

FLAT-OUT FANTASTIC

Elevated Flatbreads, Starters, and Sides

Flatbreads are technically a style of bread that is unleavened, like naan or pita. Flatbreads in the pizza world are often made with a simple (leavened) dough topped with a few ingredients (without a sauce) enjoyed as an appetizer. We use our standard Neapolitan dough as the base, and you can substitute our New York–style dough if using a grill. What makes flatbread so fun is that you can keep it as simple or complex as you want.

When it comes to a pizza night, the main star is always the pizza. But preparing a great salad and a cheese dip is easy as people arrive. You can also follow our lead and delegate the sides and appetizers to any guests coming over so that you can focus on the pizza. The Baked Breadsticks use our New York–style dough for ease of preparation and can be dipped in our Marinara, Classic Red Sauce, or Pizza Cheese Dip.

**YIELD: ONE 12-INCH
FLATBREAD**

1 pizza dough
2 tablespoons Garlic Oil
(page 105)
2 ounces fresh mozzarella,
broken up by hand into
small pieces
2 tablespoons ricotta
¼ cup grated Parmigiano-
Reggiano
¼ cup grated Asiago
1 tablespoon roughly
chopped fresh rosemary

WINE PAIRING: With four
different cheeses, garlic,
and a hint of rosemary, we
recommend something
light and crisp. Pinot gris,
vermentino, and a lighter-
bodied rosé all shine with
this flavorful flatbread.

FOUR-CHEESE FLATBREAD

When you combine four cheeses with rosemary, the world becomes a happier place, or at least the people at your home will be happy. We balance hard and soft cheeses for the best flavor combination, and the result is almost like a fancy cheesy breadstick.

- Preheat your pizza cooker to the target temperature per the instructions on pages 26 through 34.

- Form the dough into a round 11–12 inches wide on a floured surface, following the instructions on page 85.

- Move the prepared dough round to a floured pizza peel.

- On your dough round, brush the garlic oil. Layer the mozzarella and ricotta first, then sprinkle the Parmigiano-Reggiano and Asiago. Finish with the rosemary.

- Transfer the flatbread to your cooker and bake per the instructions on pages 26 through 34.

- After removing the flatbread, sprinkle with finishing salt.

GARLIC FLATBREAD

This simple garlic flatbread is perfect on its own. The rich aromas will permeate even inside the house as it comes off the grill, and the softened garlic butter provides a decadent flavor. Drizzling a touch of good olive oil on the finish adds a little more moisture and bright flavor. Make sure the garlic butter is softened and smooth enough to work with. We like to use the back of a spoon to gently spread it onto the delicate dough. This is a great appetizer to get the party started. Nothing awakens the senses quite like the smell of freshly cooked garlic and bread.

- Preheat your pizza cooker to the target temperature per the instructions on pages 26 through 34.

- Form the dough into a round 11–12 inches wide on a floured surface, following the instructions on page 85.

- Move the prepared dough round to a floured pizza peel.

- On your dough round, spread the garlic butter. Sprinkle with the cheese and rosemary.

- Transfer the flatbread to your cooker and bake per instructions on pages 26 through 34.

- After removing the flatbread, drizzle with olive oil and cut into squares. Serve warm.

YIELD: ONE 12-INCH FLATBREAD

1 pizza dough
2 tablespoons softened Magic Garlic Butter (page 104)
½ cup grated Parmigiano-Reggiano
½ teaspoon chopped fresh rosemary
2 tablespoons extra-virgin olive oil

WINE PAIRING: The citrus flavors in a crisp sauvignon blanc pair nicely with the garlic and rosemary in this simple but flavorful dish. Alternatively, grüner veltliner and albariño have the flavors and acidity that work remarkably well with the garlic and sharp cheese.

YIELD: ONE 12-INCH FLATBREAD

3 pieces Broccolini, stems trimmed

1 pizza dough

2 tablespoons extra-virgin olive oil

2 ounces fresh mozzarella, broken up by hand into small pieces

1 ounce grated Asiago

2 ounces cooked hot Italian sausage crumbles

¼ teaspoon fennel pollen

Classic Hot Honey (page 112), for drizzling

WINE PAIRING: The flavors of this flatbread are quite simple yet elegant, meant to showcase the essence of fennel pollen. Your best bet would be a *blanc de blanc* Champagne or similar-style sparkling wine. Otherwise, go with a lighter unoaked chardonnay or even Chablis. The elegant nature of these wines will be a lovely match for this flatbread.

NOTE: We do not recommend cooking fennel pollen at high heat. It will burn and taste bitter. So use (sparingly) as a finishing touch. Blanching the Broccolini provides a better texture.

FENNEL POLLEN AND HOT-HONEY FLATBREAD

When we cook at large events, we always leave inspired by the flavor combinations from other chefs. One such ingredient that is a bit hard to find, but worth the effort to seek out, is fennel pollen. This is not the same as fennel seed; it's the hand-harvested pollen from fennel. It has the essence of fennel with the aromas of citrus and bright herbs. It's best as a dusting over a dish, much like a finishing salt. It's slightly savory and adds a beautiful flavor to any dish. If you can't find fennel pollen locally, you can buy it online.

This flatbread is great with a mildly flavored vegetable, like Broccolini. Whatever you choose, give it a quick blanch or pre-roast it prior to cooking it on the flatbread.

- In a large stockpot over high heat, add the Broccolini to boiling water for 3 minutes. Remove and place in an ice bath. When cool, remove and dry.

- Preheat the pizza cooker to the target temperature per the instructions on pages 26 through 34.

- Form your dough into a round 11–12 inches wide on a floured surface, following the instructions on page 85.

- Move the prepared dough round to a floured pizza peel.

- On your dough round, brush the olive oil. Layer the mozzarella, Asiago, sausage crumbles, and blanched Broccolini.

- Transfer the flatbread to your cooker and bake per the instructions on pages 26 through 34.

- After removing the flatbread, cut into wedges and sprinkle with the fennel pollen and a drizzle of hot honey.

SUN-DRIED-TOMATO FLATBREAD

The real star of this show is the balance between the sun-dried tomato and the Asiago. Instead of loading up with a sauce, the garlic oil and cheese bring the toppings together without overpowering the flavor.

- Preheat your pizza cooker to the target temperature per the instructions on pages 26 through 34.

- Form your dough into a round 11–12 inches wide on a floured surface, following the instructions on page 85.

- Move the prepared dough round to a floured pizza peel.

- On your dough round, brush the garlic oil. Layer the sun-dried tomatoes, rosemary, Asiago, and mozzarella.

- Transfer the flatbread to your cooker and bake per the instructions on pages 26 through 34.

- After removing the flatbread, set on a cutting board and sprinkle with finishing salt.

YIELD: ONE 12-INCH FLATBREAD

1 pizza dough
2 tablespoons Garlic Oil (page 105)
⅓ cup chopped sun-dried tomatoes, drained of excess oil
1 teaspoon chopped fresh rosemary
¼ cup grated Asiago
¼ cup fresh mozzarella, broken up by hand into small pieces
Pinch of finishing salt

WINE PAIRING: Sun-dried tomatoes live in a world that balances sweet and savory with a full load of concentrated flavor. When combining the sun-dried tomatoes with a sharp Asiago, we love a bright acidic Chianti (made from sangiovese grapes) for its earthy, cherry, and leathery notes.

PIZZA CHEESE DIP

Equipment:

One 6-inch deep-dish pan
or cast-iron pan

8 ounces cream cheese,
softened

1 cup grated Parmigiano-
Reggiano, divided

½ cup shredded low-
moisture mozzarella,
divided

¼ teaspoon kosher salt

¼ teaspoon dried oregano,
plus more for dusting

½ cup Marinara (page 107)

8 pepperoni slices

Red pepper flakes,
for dusting

8 Baked Breadsticks
(page 127)

WINE PAIRING: The dip's
richness and creaminess
coat the palate, meaning
you need a wine with high
acidity to cut through and
refresh. Cava, sparkling
wine from Spain, is a great
candidate for the job, as is
Prosecco from Italy. If you
want something still, reach
for an albariño or even a
pinot blanc. They won't pack
quite the punch, but they'll
sure be tasty.

Sean has a regular guys' night with a good friend of his at a local
taproom. This dip is inspired by an appetizer from there, and
it's apparently the only thing they ever eat while sipping beers
and catching up on life and kids. Mary has never been invited to
this sacred meeting of the boys, so she had to take Sean's word
that this is a close match to his favorite appetizer. The simple
combination of cream cheese and pizza ingredients makes it a
great cheesy comfort-food dip. It's also easy to scale up for a crowd.

- Preheat the grill or pizza oven to 500 degrees F. The stone should not
  exceed 550 degrees F.

- In a large bowl, combine the cream cheese, half of both the Parmigiano-
  Reggiano and mozzarella, salt, and oregano.

- In the deep-dish pan, spread out the cheese mixture with a spatula.
  Layer the marinara and remaining cheeses, and top with the pepperoni.
  Sprinkle with red pepper flakes and oregano.

- Place pan on the stone and cook for up to 10 minutes, or until the
  cheese is bubbling and the pepperoni has crisped up.

- After removing the cheese dip, let it sit for 5 minutes. Serve warm
  with breadsticks.

CHEF'S TIP: If using a pizza oven, you will need to rotate the cheese
dip with your turning peel every 30 seconds. Be sure the flame is not
too large.

BAKED BREADSTICKS

Breadsticks are only as good as the dough that makes them. We like to use our New York–style dough for the extra chew and weight. It's a little work to bake them on a grill or in a pizza oven, but worth it. Alternatively, you can bake these in your kitchen oven at 425 degrees F on a sheet pan lined with parchment paper.

- Preheat the grill to 425 degrees F. The pizza stone should not exceed 425 degrees F.

- After the dough has proofed during second fermentation, divide it into eight equal parts.

- Roll out the dough into 5-inch-long strings with the palm of your hand. It's best that the dough is room temperature; otherwise, it will shrink.

- If you are not baking right away, place parchment paper on a sheet tray and lay out the breadsticks. Cover with plastic wrap and let sit at room temperature. If you are making them the next day, store them in the refrigerator. They will continue to rise.

- When ready to bake, remove the breadsticks from the refrigerator and coat the tops with the garlic oil. Sprinkle with the cheese. Place the breadsticks on a floured peel.

- Bake directly on the stone for up to 8 minutes. If using a pizza oven, you'll need to rotate the breadsticks 180 degrees after 4 minutes for even cooking.

- Serve with the thick marinara or pizza cheese dip.

YIELD: 8 BREADSTICKS

1 pizza dough (280 g) (we recommend the All-Purpose New York–Inspired Dough, page 100)

2 tablespoons Garlic Oil (page 105)

½ teaspoon grated Parmigiano-Reggiano

Marinara (page 107) or Pizza Cheese Dip (page 124), for dipping

WINE PAIRING: Breadsticks are like an aperitif to a party, best snacked on while the main course is cooking. Therefore, the wines should follow suit. Reach for something light and festive that you would drink while guests are rolling in, like bubbly or pinot gris. These fruity, lively wines are great with garlicky bready snacks.

YIELD: 4 CUPS SALAD

For the croutons:

2 cups freshly grated
    Parmigiano-Reggiano

3 tablespoons ranch
    seasoning powder

For the salad dressing:

3 tablespoons freshly grated
    Parmigiano-Reggiano

2 garlic cloves, crushed

1 teaspoon anchovy paste

½ teaspoon kosher salt

½ teaspoon coarse
    black pepper

¼ cup freshly squeezed
    lemon juice (about
    ½ a lemon)

2 egg yolks

½ teaspoon Dijon mustard

½ cup extra-virgin olive oil

2 hearts of romaine
    lettuce, chopped

WINE PAIRING: An excellent
Caesar salad is all about the
dressing. It should have a
good bite and a nice tang,
with the signature flavors of
the anchovy paste, Dijon,
and lemon. Our favorite
pairings include zesty, crisp
wines, such as unoaked
chardonnays, chenin blanc,
and even vermentino.
Rosés work quite well
too, especially with those
savory croutons.

CAESAR SALAD
with Parmesan-Ranch Baked Croutons

In addition to a great dressing, this salad adds amazing croutons.
We learned about this flavor hack from Chef Britt Rescigno and
Kinsey Leodler, of Communion Bay Supper Club in Sun Valley,
Idaho, when we cooked with them at a food and wine event.
Instead of boring stale croutons, they mixed freshly grated
Parmigiano-Reggiano with dry ranch powder and pork rinds. We
skipped the pork rinds (you don't have to) and gave it our twist.
The look of awe people give you when you serve them this salad
will have you making it on the regular.

- Preheat your oven to 350 degrees F.

- To make the croutons, in a medium-size bowl, combine Parmigiano-
  Reggiano and ranch seasoning.

- Arrange the cheese mix in one even layer on parchment paper or a
  Silpat sheet.

- Bake in the center rack for no more than 8 minutes, or until the cheese
  is golden brown.

- After removing the cheese, let it cool to crisp up and harden. Break
  the cheese into pieces, or croutons. (They can be made up to 3 days in
  advance if stored in an airtight container.)

- To make the salad dressing: In a food processor, add the Parmigiano-
  Reggiano, garlic, anchovy paste, salt, and pepper. Pulse until the mixture
  forms a paste. Add the lemon juice, egg yolks, mustard, and olive oil.
  Blend on low until it emulsifies, which will take at least a minute.

- In a large bowl, toss the romaine lettuce with the dressing, and gently
  fold in the Parmesan croutons.

KEEPING IT CLASSY
Classic Pizzas Everyone Should Know

These classic pizzas reflect the originals that in turn reflect a certain style or region from Italy to New York to Chicago and to our very own Pacific Northwest. With every recipe, we try to honor the specific flavors of the classic pizzas because there's a reason they are timeless.

YIELD: ONE 12-INCH PIZZA

1 Neapolitan-Style Dough
(page 98)
¼ cup of Neapolitan-
Inspired Red Sauce
(page 106)
¼ cup fresh mozzarella,
broken up by hand
into chunks
5 to 6 fresh basil leaves
Pinch of finishing salt
Extra-virgin olive oil,
for drizzling

WINE PAIRING: Simple
meets sublime. This classic
pizza's elegance calls for a
wine that's equally refined
while keeping things
simple. With its bright
acidity and cherry-forward
flavors, a Chianti Classico
(made predominantly
from sangiovese grapes)
blends harmoniously with
the tangy tomato sauce
and creamy mozzarella.
Other lightweight reds work
equally great, like pinot
noir, Beaujolais (made from
gamay noir grapes), or rosé
(especially those from Italy).

MARGHERITA

This is the queen of pizzas and the first one we make anytime
we throw a pizza party. It's the benchmark of a good party and a
great one to get you warmed up before you begin making more
adventurous pizzas. Work with the very best quality ingredients,
and you're off to a promising start.

- Preheat your pizza cooker to the target temperature per the instructions
  on pages 26 through 34.

- Form the dough into a round 11–12 inches wide on a floured surface,
  following the instructions on page 85.

- Move the prepared dough round to a floured pizza peel.

- Spread the sauce evenly over the dough to within ½ inch of the rim.
  Then layer the mozzarella and top with basil leaves.

- Transfer the pizza to your cooker and bake per the instructions on pages
  26 through 34.

- After removing pizza to a cutting board, dust with finishing salt and
  drizzle with olive oil. Cut into wedges and serve warm.

NOTE: If you want a nod to the true Italian margherita pizza, be sure your
mozzarella is cut into even pieces and evenly distributed around the pizza.
Drizzle with olive oil before cooking.

NEW YORK–STYLE PEPPERONI

This one is all about the right crust and pepperoni that curls up into "cups" and holds the fat and flavor. This classic will never go out of style. People travel to New York just to eat this pizza. But guess what? You only have to travel to your backyard to get the same flavor experience. We buy a whole pepperoni log and slice it thin for the best results and cupping. And don't you dare blot the pizza with a paper towel. That fat is flavor.

- Preheat your pizza cooker to the target temperature per the instructions on pages 26 through 34. However, given this is a New York–style pizza, we recommend the pizza stone reach 500 degrees F.

- Form the dough into a round 11–12 inches wide on a floured surface, following the instructions on page 85.

- Move the prepared dough round to a floured pizza peel.

- On your pizza round, layer the sauce and cheese, and then add the pepperoni.

- Transfer the pizza to your cooker and bake per instructions on pages 26 through 34.

- After removing the pizza, sprinkle with the oregano and red pepper flakes. Cut into slices. If you want to look like a true New Yorker, fold your slice in half to eat.

YIELD: ONE 12-INCH PIZZA

1 All-Purpose New York–Inspired Dough (page 100)

½ cup Classic Red Sauce (page 107)

⅓ cup shredded low-moisture mozzarella

⅓ cup thinly sliced pepperoni

1 teaspoon dried oregano

1 teaspoon red pepper flakes

WINE PAIRING: A bold syrah is a great partner for this meaty masterpiece. Its robust tannins and dark berry flavors stand up solidly to the rich savory meats, while the peppery and spice notes complement the spiciness of the pepperoni. Cabernet franc is a close second favorite.

1 tablespoon extra-virgin
    olive oil

½ cup thinly sliced shiitake
    mushrooms

1 pizza dough

⅓ cup Basic White Sauce
    (page 108)

½ cup caramelized onions
    (recipe follows)

2 ounces fresh mozzarella,
    broken up by hand into
    chunks

¼ cup ricotta

Pinch of finishing salt

¼ cup arugula (optional)

WINE PAIRING: We're
huge fans of a full-bodied
chardonnay for this deeply
flavored pizza. With the
pizza's creamy sauce, earthy
mushrooms, and cheeses,
the weight of chardonnay
will match well and its
brightness will help cut
through the richness of the
pizza. Viognier would be a
close second.

CLASSIC WHITE PIZZA
with Caramelized Onions

This is a flavor bomb of creamy-cheesy-savory proportions. The combination of the caramelized onions, earthy mushrooms, and cheeses is enough to excite any vegetarian or carnivore alike.

- In a small saucepan over medium heat, add the olive oil and shiitake mushrooms. Allow to brown for 3–4 minutes before stirring them. Then stir and continue to brown for an additional 3–4 minutes to soften and cook them down. Remove and set aside.

- Preheat your pizza cooker to the target temperature per the instructions on pages 26 through 34.

- Form the dough into a round 11–12 inches wide on a floured surface, following the instructions on page 85.

- Move the prepared dough round to a floured pizza peel.

- Spread the white sauce evenly over the dough to within ½ inch of the rim. Layer with the mushrooms, onions, and cheeses.

- Transfer the pizza to your cooker and bake per the instructions on pages 26 through 34.

- After removing the pizza, sprinkle with finishing salt and arugula. Cut into wedges and serve.

NOTE: Ricotta is sticky and wet. We drop small dollops (about 1 teaspoon portions) by hand evenly over the pizza, as if placing pieces of pepperoni.

Caramelized Onions

1 tablespoon unsalted butter   1 medium onion, thinly sliced
1 tablespoon extra-virgin olive oil   ¼ teaspoon kosher salt

Let's get right to the point: most people don't caramelize their onions enough. The water needs to be completely cooked out of them before they start to brown. You can find a video tutorial at Vindulge.com. These can be made up to 3 days in advance.

- In a small saucepan over medium heat, add the butter and olive oil, then the onions.

- Decrease the heat to medium-low and cook for up to 30 minutes, stirring occasionally. If you don't hear the onions sizzling, increase the heat. The onions will reduce, brown, and get slightly crispy. Salt at the end as you turn off the heat.

GOAT CHEESE AND MUSHROOM PIZZA

Goat cheese and mushrooms work so beautifully together and are often seen on many pizzeria menus around the country. The goat cheese melts slightly but still retains its dense texture. For any of our mushroom pizzas, we recommend browning the shrooms first. Raw mushrooms on pizzas don't have the same flavor.

- In a cast-iron pan over medium heat, melt the butter. Add half the mushrooms and stir occasionally until browned. Remove and set aside, then repeat with the remaining half of the mushrooms.

- Preheat your pizza cooker to the target temperature per the instructions on pages 26 through 34.

- Form the dough into a round 11–12 inches wide on a floured surface, following the instructions on page 85.

- Move the prepared dough round to a floured pizza peel.

- On your pizza round, drizzle the Garlic Oil and then spread with the backside of a large spoon to within ½ inch of the rim. Spread the white sauce evenly in the same manner. Layer with the mushrooms and chunks of the goat cheese.

- Transfer the pizza to your cooker and bake per the instructions on pages 26 through 34.

- After removing the pizza, sprinkle with finishing salt. Cut into wedges and serve.

CHEF'S TIP: You don't want to overcrowd the mushrooms because they are mostly water. If the pan is too crowded, the mushrooms will steam and not brown.

YIELD: ONE 12-INCH PIZZA

2 tablespoons unsalted butter
2 ounces cremini mushrooms, sliced
2 ounces shiitake mushrooms, sliced
2 ounces oyster mushrooms, roughly chopped
1 pizza dough
2 tablespoons Garlic Oil (page 105)
⅓ cup Basic White Sauce (page 108)
2 ounces goat cheese (¼ cup)
Pinch of finishing salt

WINE PAIRING: Sauvignon blanc, particularly from the Loire Valley of France, is delicious with goat cheese. If you want a red, try a lighter-style cabernet franc or even a pinot noir. They're a great match for the earthy mushrooms.

**YIELD: ONE 10-INCH
CAST-IRON PIZZA**

Equipment:
10-inch cast-iron pan or
  deep-dish pizza pan

1 tablespoon unsalted butter
1 pizza dough (600–620 g)
6 slices provolone
6 slices (or 1 heaping cup
  shredded) low-moisture
  mozzarella
½ pound ground Italian
  sausage
½ cup diced green bell
  pepper
1½ cups Marinara (page 107)
¼ cup grated Parmigiano-
  Reggiano

WINE PAIRING: This is a
big and rich pizza, laden
with layers of cheese,
spicy sausage, and a thick
red sauce. Let's go with
something to match the
richness: syrah. This is a
strong match for the fennel-
driven spicy sausage, and
has good tannins and acidity
to stand up to the cheeses
and acidic sauce. Similarly,
you could choose a rich
mourvèdre or grenache.
Both would be delicious!

DEEP-DISH PIZZA

The inspiration for this pizza is definitely Chicago. Making deep-dish pizza can be a technical challenge in a pizza oven due to the amount of time it takes to bake a Chicago-style crust. We recommend baking this pizza on a grill to give the crust time to firm up and to allow the pizza to cook all the way through. It also needs more dough than our typical pizzas.

When making the dough, and going through the second rise, instead of dividing into three dough balls, we divide into two. The first dough ball will weigh about 280 grams (perfect for all the individual pizzas in this book), and the second (a double size) will be a little over 600 grams. Knead, form, and rise the second ball the same way; it just weighs more and will be able to stretch out for the size of the pan.

- Preheat your grill so the pizza stone reaches 500 degrees F.

- Form the dough into a round 13 inches wide on a floured surface, following the instructions on page 85.

- Move the prepared dough round to a well-buttered 10-inch cast-iron pan. Press the dough into the base and up along the sides of the pan.

- Layer the provolone slices, overlapping them. Do the same with the mozzarella. Add small chunks of the sausage, followed by the bell pepper. Cover with the sauce, evening it out with the back of a spoon. Sprinkle the Parmigiano-Reggiano over the sauce.

- If there is excess dough hanging off the edges of the pan, remove it with a knife and pinch the excess dough over the rim so it doesn't shrink back.

- Transfer the pizza to your grill and bake for up to 25 minutes. The dough should be browned and slightly pulled back from the edges of the pan.

- After removing the pizza, let it rest for 10 minutes. Then, using a large spatula and your hands, carefully transfer the pie from the pan onto a cutting board. Cut into wedges and enjoy.

A
SAVORY SYMPHONY
Harmonizing Flavors

When planning a pizza party, we like to pick from a variety of options to balance out a crowd. Savory pizzas are typically the most common outside the classics. These pizzas have a flavor profile driven by savory and rich ingredients, which may not always mean meat.

---

1 pizza dough
2 tablespoons Garlic Oil
    (page 105)
⅓ cup Marinara Sauce
    (page 107)
½ cup grated pecorino
    Romano
⅓ cup fresh basil
Pinch of finishing salt
Extra-virgin olive oil,
    for drizzling

WINE PAIRING: Pop open
a bottle of Chianti Classico
for this bad boy. The
bright, fruity notes of this
Tuscan red complement
the freshness of the
pomodoro sauce, creating
a symphony of flavors that
will delight your palate
with each bite. This flavor
combination pairs well with
wines that have elegance
yet simplicity. Alternatively,
pinot grigio is also a lovely
match if you're looking for
something light and bright.

THE POMODORO PIZZA

Bursting with the fresh flavors of ripe tomatoes, aromatic garlic, and fragrant basil, this is a celebration of simplicity and quality ingredients. Elevate pizza night by following this minimalist yet irresistible recipe, and savor the delectable marriage of fresh ingredients atop each slice. This recipe is all about the sauce and simplicity. Instead of making a new sauce, full of fragrant garlic, we just layer some garlic oil with the Marinara to give it depth.

- Preheat your pizza cooker to the target temperature per the instructions on pages 26 through 34.

- Form the dough into a round 11–12 inches wide on a floured surface, following the instructions on page 85.

- Move the prepared dough round to a floured pizza peel.

- On your pizza round, brush on olive oil, then layer the sauce, cheese, and basil.

- Transfer the pizza to your cooker and bake per the instructions on pages 26 through 34.

- After removing the pizza, sprinkle with finishing salt and drizzle with olive oil. Cut into wedges and serve.

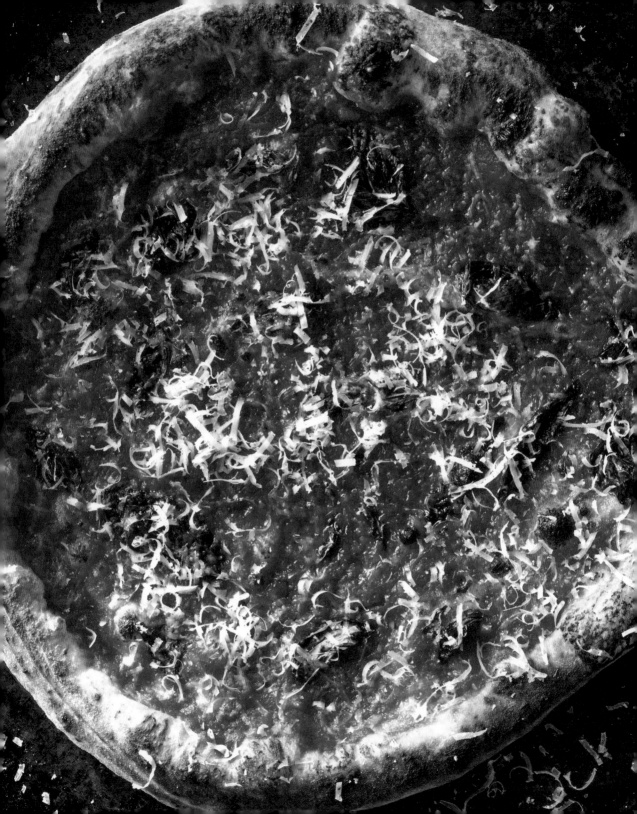

PESTO SAUSAGE

When the vibrant flavors of pesto meet spicy sausage, this pizza becomes a flavor explosion in the best possible way. Vindulge in a culinary masterpiece that transforms the ordinary into an extraordinary pizza experience, a lovely balance that will leave your taste buds craving for more.

- In a small saucepan over medium heat, melt the butter and olive oil. Add the mushrooms and allow them to brown for 5 minutes before stirring. Then stir and continue to brown for an additional 5 minutes. Remove and set aside.

- Preheat your pizza cooker to the target temperature per the instructions on pages 26 through 34.

- Form the dough into a round 11–12 inches wide on a floured surface, following the instructions on page 85.

- Move the prepared dough round to a floured pizza peel.

- On your pizza round, layer the pesto to within ½ inch of the rim, and then add the mushrooms, sausage, and mozzarella.

- Transfer the pizza to your cooker and bake per the instructions on pages 26 through 34.

- After removing the pizza, sprinkle with finishing salt.

YIELD: ONE 12-INCH PIZZA

1 tablespoon unsalted butter
1 tablespoon extra-virgin olive oil
3 ounces cremini mushrooms, sliced
1 pizza dough
⅓ cup Hazelnut Pesto (page 109)
½ cup cooked and crumbled hot Italian sausage
¼ cup fresh mozzarella, broken up by hand into chunks
Pinch of finishing salt

WINE PAIRING:
Complement this delicious creation with a crisp sauvignon blanc or verdicchio; the bright acidity and citrus notes will enhance the richness of the sausage while harmonizing with the herbal flavors of the pesto. Alternatively, syrah is great with the spicy sausage and mushrooms and works surprisingly well with the pesto.

¼ cup Classic Red Sauce
  (page 107)
1 tablespoon hoisin sauce
1 tablespoon sriracha
1 pizza dough
⅓ cup shredded low-
  moisture mozzarella
½ cup thinly sliced
  pineapple chunks
2 ounces cooked pancetta
  (about ¼ cup)
3 prosciutto slices
⅓ cup thinly sliced sweet
  onion (white)
Pinch of finishing salt

WINE PAIRING: A
slightly sweet riesling is
(dare we say) a match
made in pizzeria heaven
when combined with the
pineapple and savory
pancetta. The acidity in
the wine brightens the
palate after a bite of the
rich sauce and balances
the complexity of flavors
in this pizza. Lambrusco
is another win for this
flavor bomb of a meal.

THE CONTROVERSIAL PINEAPPLE

Out of all the possible recipes in the world, this is the one pizza our kids requested be in the book, despite a classic pepperoni being their favorite pizza. At their young age, they already know about the divisive nature of pineapple on a pizza. They must be destined to be troublemakers. When we want to try a unique flavor profile on a pizza, we often add some different ingredients into our Classic Red Sauce so that it has that traditional taste, but with something extra. Here, we mix hoisin and sriracha into the red sauce. It's a delicious combination that pairs well with the savory meat and sweet pineapple, so even the haters might get on board.

- Combine the red sauce, hoisin sauce, and sriracha in a small bowl. Set aside and let the flavors integrate.

- Preheat your pizza cooker to the target temperature per the instructions on pages 26 through 34.

- Form the dough into a round 11–12 inches wide on a floured surface, following the instructions on page 85.

- Move the prepared dough round to a floured pizza peel.

- On your pizza round, layer the sauce, cheese, pineapple, pancetta, prosciutto, and onion.

- Transfer the pizza to your cooker and bake per the instructions on pages 26 through 34.

- After removing the pizza, sprinkle with finishing salt.

THE DIAVOLA PIZZA

Named after the Italian word for "devil," this pizza offers a spicy kick, something that promises quite the experience for the adventurous. We first encountered this style at a Portland, Oregon, pizzeria, and it quickly became a favorite. It usually features a combination of spicy meats and chili peppers; our version involves a mix of meats and is topped with our favorite spicy condiment, Mama Lil's Peppers. Mama Lil's uses Hungarian "Goathorn" peppers; if you can't find them, look for a similar style of spicy pickled pepper packed in oil.

- Preheat your pizza cooker to the target temperature per the instructions on pages 26 through 34.

- Form the dough into a round 11–12 inches wide on a floured surface, following the instructions on page 85.

- Move the prepared dough round to a floured pizza peel.

- On your pizza round, layer the sauce, mozzarella, soppressata, coppa, and pickled peppers.

- Transfer the pizza to your cooker and bake per the instructions on pages 26 through 34.

- After removing the pizza, sprinkle with finishing salt.

YIELD: ONE 12-INCH PIZZA

1 pizza dough
⅓ cup Classic Red Sauce (page 107)
3 ounces fresh mozzarella, broken up by hand into small pieces
4 slices thinly cut soppressata
4 slices thinly cut coppa
¼ cup diced Mama Lil's Peppers
A pinch of finishing salt (such as Maldon)

WINE PAIRING: Every time we eat this pizza, we are drawn to a fruity, refreshing rosé or arneis. This pizza is a flavor explosion (in the best possible way), and needs something to cool and cleanse the palate from the spicy peppers and meats. Rosé has never let me down. But if you're not scared of a little boldness, reach for a wine that packs a punch. Try a richer-style syrah, merlot, or even a zinfandel if you're in the mood for a red that stands up to the devil himself.

DATE-NIGHT STEAK DINNER PIZZA

A perfectly grilled steak is a thing of beauty. Add thin slices to a pizza with a chimichurri base and layers of creamy melted blue cheese, and this becomes pure date-night decadence on a pizza! We recommend that you cook this one on your grill, since you'll already be grilling your steak. Once the steak is done and resting, add the stone, let it warm up, and cook the pizza directly on the same grill.

When cooking the steak, remove it while it's still rare. It will continue cooking after you slice it and will finish on the pizza. The key is to not overcook it.

- Prepare your grill for direct grilling, targeting 450 degrees F.

- Season the steak with the Beef Seasoning and grill over direct heat. Grill each side of the steak for 4 minutes, turning it until the steak reaches an internal temperature of 110 degrees F (rare).

- Remove the steak from the grill and let rest for 15 minutes. (It will continue cooking on the pizza.)

- Thinly slice the steak.

- Adjust grill for baking your pizza based on the instructions on pages 26 through 34 for your specific grill.

- Form the dough into a round 11–12 inches wide on a floured surface, following the instructions on page 85.

- Move the prepared dough round to a floured pizza peel.

$\longrightarrow$

YIELD: ONE 12-INCH PIZZA

⅔ pounds hanger steak

2 tablespoons Beef Seasoning (recipe follows)

1 pizza dough

¼ cup Easy Chimichurri, plus more for finishing (page 113)

3 ounces creamy blue cheese, sliced into thin strips (look for a soft wedge instead of blue cheese crumbles)

¼ cup thinly sliced red onion

Pinch of finishing salt

WINE PAIRING: Classic steak-night dinner wines do well here. A rich malbec or cabernet sauvignon stand up to the flavorful steak and creamy blue cheese. Carménère is another one that pairs well with chimichurri. Pour two glasses and enjoy date-night bliss!

continued from previous page

- On your pizza round, spread the chimichurri to within ½ inch of the rim. Then layer with the sliced steak, blue cheese strips, and red onion.

- Transfer the pizza to your grill and bake per the instructions on pages 26 through 34.

- After removing the pizza, sprinkle with finishing salt and a light drizzle of more chimichurri.

Beef Seasoning

YIELD: JUST UNDER 1 CUP

¼ cup kosher salt
¼ cup coarse black pepper
2 tablespoons paprika
2 tablespoons crushed dried
   rosemary

1 tablespoon dried thyme
1 tablespoon dried mustard
1 tablespoon red pepper flakes

- Combine the salt, pepper, paprika, rosemary, thyme, mustard, and red pepper flakes and store in a mason jar for up to 6 months.

BBQ PULLED-PORK PIZZA

If you own a smoker or grill, we expect you to have some pulled pork leftover from time to time. This is a great way to use it up! Pork dries out in the fridge, so we like to warm it up and rehydrate it in a pan with some BBQ sauce or apple cider vinegar before adding it to the pizza. Use your favorite Kansas City–style BBQ sauce as a base (or opt for our Pinot Noir BBQ Sauce, found at Vindulge.com), and build your masterpiece. We recommend you cook this one on the grill, as it is a little heavier than what we like for a dedicated pizza oven and cooks a little slower, which integrates the flavors.

- Preheat your grill to the target temperature per the instructions on pages 26 through 34.

- In a small saucepan over medium heat, add 2 tablespoons of the BBQ sauce and the leftover pulled pork. Stir to warm up and rehydrate, about 6 minutes.

- Form the dough into a round 11–12 inches wide on a floured surface, following the instructions on page 85.

- Move the prepared dough round to a floured pizza peel.

- On your pizza round, spread the BBQ sauce to within ½ inch of the rim, then layer the pulled pork, cheeses, jalapeños, and onion.

- Transfer the pizza to your grill and bake per the instructions on pages 26 through 34.

- After removing the pizza, sprinkle with the cilantro and finishing salt.

NOTE: Warm up the pulled pork in advance so it's not blazing hot when you add it to the pizza. If it's too hot, it will warm your dough and make it stick to the peel. It's a fine balance to warm and rehydrate the pork without making it too hot.

YIELD: ONE 12-INCH PIZZA

⅓ cup Kansas City–style BBQ sauce, plus 2 tablespoons
¾ cup leftover shredded pulled pork
1 pizza dough (we recommend the All-Purpose New York–Inspired Dough (page 100)
⅓ cup shredded low-moisture mozzarella
⅓ cup grated sharp cheddar
¼ cup Quick Pickle Jalapeños (recipe follows)
¼ cup thinly sliced red onion
¼ cup chopped cilantro
Pinch of finishing salt

WINE PAIRING: Classic BBQ flavors call for a classic wine pairing. The smoky and savory pork, along with the rich BBQ sauce, is always a great match for bold, fruity wines like syrah or zinfandel.

$\longrightarrow$

Quick Pickle Jalapeños

½ cup water
¼ cup white vinegar

¼ cup cane sugar
½ cup thinly sliced jalapeños

- In a small saucepan over medium heat, combine the water, vinegar, and sugar. Stir and bring to a simmer. Add the jalapeños and simmer for 10 minutes. Turn off the heat and let rest for 10 minutes. Store in a mason jar in the refrigerator for up to 10 days.

WHITE TRUFFLE AND THREE-CHEESE PIZZA

Get ready for a night on the town with this flavor fiesta of a pizza. This cheesy affair is going to make your taste buds dance the night away, but you don't need to venture to a fancy restaurant or club to treat yourself to the irresistible essence of truffle oil. You can bring the glitz and glamour to your backyard with an all-star ensemble of cheeses, enticing herbs, and the luxurious touch of black truffle oil. Your guests will feel like VIPs in the comfort of your own backyard.

- Preheat your pizza cooker to the target temperature per the instructions on pages 26 through 34.

- Form your dough into a round 11–12 inches wide on a floured surface, following the instructions on page 85.

- Move the prepared dough round to a floured pizza peel.

- On your pizza round, brush the olive oil and layer the cheeses and rosemary.

- Transfer the pizza to your cooker and bake per the instructions on pages 26 through 34.

- After removing the pizza, add the black pepper and a drizzle of the truffle oil. Cut into wedges and serve immediately.

YIELD: ONE 12-INCH PIZZA

1 pizza dough

1 tablespoon extra-virgin olive oil

1 ounce grated Asiago

2 ounces fresh mozzarella, broken up by hand into small chunks

2 ounces ricotta, separated by hand into small chunks

1 teaspoon chopped fresh rosemary

3 turns of freshly cracked black pepper

1 tablespoon black truffle oil

WINE PAIRING:
Complement the lavish flavors of the black truffle oil and the rich cheeses with an oaked chardonnay. The wine's textures, bright citrus, and ripe fruit provide a lovely counterpoint to the rich truffle oil and creamy cheese, resulting in a thing of beauty. For red, pinot noir works equally well to create a harmony of flavors.

3 tablespoons fig preserves
or fig jam

1 pizza dough

2 ounces Brie with the rind
on, cut into 2-inch-long
slices

2 slices prosciutto, broken
up by hand into smaller
pieces

½ teaspoon aged balsamic
vinegar

1 teaspoon chopped fresh
rosemary

¼ teaspoon red pepper
flakes

Arugula, for sprinkling

WINE PAIRING: The
concentrated flavor of the
jam, combined with the
richness of the cheese
and delicate nature of the
prosciutto, has us craving
a Provence-style rosé or
even the slight sweetness
of prosecco. It also feels
right with the cocktail-party
theme. Yum.

FIG AND PROSCIUTTO
with Brie

This pizza is basically the cool kid at a charcuterie party. All
the great things that adorn a typical meat and cheese board are
combined, creating a delicious intersection of indulgence. Instead
of hovering near the table, picking at your favorites, just layer the
fig jam, slices of creamy Brie, and melt-in-your-mouth prosciutto,
cook to perfection, and finish with a drizzle of aged balsamic.
Pizza night just got a cocktail-party upgrade! Boom.

- Preheat your pizza cooker to the target temperature per the instructions on
  pages 26 through 34.

- Place the fig preserves in a small bowl and mix with a fork to loosen so it
  becomes spreadable.

- Form the dough into a round 11–12 inches wide on a floured surface, following
  the instructions on page 85.

- Move the prepared dough round to a floured pizza peel.

- On your pizza round, spread the fig jam to within ½ inch of the rim and top
  with the Brie and prosciutto. Shake the pizza on the peel to make sure it
  slides.

- Transfer the pizza to your cooker and bake per the instructions on pages 26
  through 34.

- After removing the pizza, add the balsamic vinegar, rosemary, and red
  pepper flakes. Garnish with arugula. Cut into wedges and serve immediately.

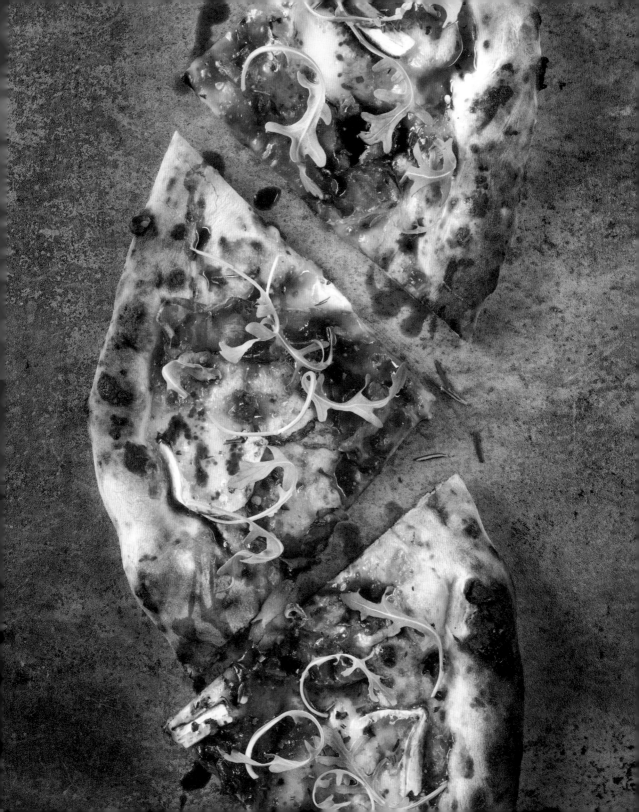

A VEGGIE VOYAGE

Our vegetarian pizzas are meant to bring big flavor. Even the meat lovers in your life will devour these. We like to balance a great sauce base with rich, savory cheeses or mushrooms as well as a touch of acid to finish. Get creative, but remember the rule: do not overload that pizza!

1 pizza dough
⅓ cup Hazelnut Pesto (page 109)
⅓ cup grated pecorino Romano
¼ cup shredded low-moisture mozzarella
1 tablespoon Classic Hot Honey (page 112)
1 cup fresh arugula
Squeeze of fresh lemon juice, for drizzling

WINE PAIRING: The zesty, herbaceous qualities of a sauvignon blanc beautifully mirror the basil in the pesto. Its crisp acidity and bright citrus notes provide a refreshing contrast to the richness of the cheeses, creating a lively and invigorating pairing.

PESTO
with Arugula

We really dig this combination. It seems simple, but this pizza is like a flavor-packed garden party on a pizza crust. Layered with the finger-licking goodness of our Hazelnut Pesto, topped with peppery arugula, and finished with a kiss of hot honey, this style will have your taste buds dancing barefoot in the grass.

- Preheat the pizza cooker to your target temperature per the instructions on pages 26 through 34.

- Form your dough into a round 11–12 inches wide on a floured surface, following the instructions on page 85.

- Move the prepared dough round to a floured pizza peel.

- On your pizza round, layer the pesto and cheeses.

- Transfer the pizza to your cooker and bake per the instructions on pages 26 through 34.

- After removing the pizza, drizzle with the hot honey, cover with arugula, and finish with a squeeze of lemon juice. Cut into wedges and serve.

YIELD: ONE 12-INCH PIZZA

1 tablespoon unsalted
butter

1 tablespoon extra-virgin
olive oil

3 ounces shiitake
mushrooms, sliced

3 ounces chanterelle
mushrooms, sliced

1 pizza dough

⅓ cup Neapolitan-Inspired
Red Sauce (page 106)

3 ounces fresh mozzarella,
broken up by hand into
smaller pieces

¼ cup grated pecorino
Romano

WINE PAIRING: Just as
adventurous Oregonians
will demand to forage for
their own locally grown
mushrooms on a blustery,
gray and wet day, they will
also request pinot noir from
Oregon to drink with their
earthy, savory meal. It really
is a match made in heaven,
or rather the forest.

THE FORAGER PIZZA

Brave Oregonians are known to venture into the woods and
handpick their own mushrooms. It's a thing. But if you're like us,
and would prefer to do your shopping at the farmers' market or
grocery store, we've still got great options.

You can use a mix of mushrooms for this pizza. We
recommend a combination of shiitakes, chanterelles, and porcini,
if you can find them. You can also substitute portobello or cremini
if you must. The key is to have a mix of savory mushrooms.

- Preheat your pizza cooker to the target temperature per the instructions
  on pages 26 through 34.

- In a small saucepan over medium heat, add the butter, olive oil, and
  mushrooms. Allow them to brown for 5 minutes before stirring. Then
  stir and continue to brown for an additional 5 minutes. Remove and
  set aside.

- Form the dough into a round 11–12 inches wide on a floured surface,
  following the instructions on page 85.

- Move the prepared dough round to a floured pizza peel.

- On your pizza round, spread the sauce within ½ inch of the rim, then add
  the mushrooms. Top with the cheeses.

- Transfer the pizza to your cooker and bake per instructions on pages 26
  through 34.

- After removing the pizza, cut into wedges and serve.

LOADED FIRE-ROASTED VEGGIE SUPREME PIZZA

Remember the rule about not overloading a pizza? Well, Mary is notorious for breaking the rules. So while we adamantly request you don't overload your pizzas, the little deviant voice in her head hears, "Challenge accepted." This is an ode to Mary and how she found a work-around for adding as many toppings as her vegetable-loving heart desires. The key here is to parbake the dough, after grilling the veggies, to give it a solid base.

We recommend everything be cooked on the grill for this pizza. Grill the veggies, prep the dough, parbake the dough solo, then add the toppings, and finish back on the grill. The vegetables have lots of moisture, so keep the cheese low-moisture to avoid adding excess liquid to the pizza. Trust us on this one!

- On a sheet pan, coat the zucchini, bell pepper, onion, and portobello with the olive oil. Season with the salt and pepper and toss.

- Grill the veggies over direct heat at 500 degrees F until all sides are browned (about 9 minutes). Some of the veggies will be done sooner, so remove when browned. Slice the portobello and bell pepper into thin strips.

- Form the dough into a round 11–12 inches wide on a floured surface, following the instructions on page 85.

- Move the prepared dough round to a floured pizza peel.

1 small zucchini, sliced into medallions about ¼ inch thick

1 orange or yelllow bell pepper, quartered

½ medium onion, thickly sliced rounds

1 portobello mushroom

3 tablespoons extra-virgin olive oil

½ teaspoon kosher salt

½ teaspoon coarse black pepper

1 pizza dough (we recommend the All-Purpose New York–Inspired Dough, page 100)

½ cup Classic Red Sauce (page 107)

⅓ cup shredded low-moisture mozzarella

⅓ cup grated pecorino Romano

¼ cup cherry tomatoes, halved

WINE PAIRING: Veggie lovers unite! We've got an array assembled: the earthy mushroom, grilled zucchini, sweet bell peppers, onion, and tomatoes. For whites wines, sauvignon blanc and chenin blanc stand up well to the flavors here. For reds, don't go too big; stick to lighter, fruity wines like pinot noir or even Chianti (made with sangiovese grapes).

→

continued from previous page

- Once veggies are removed, place the dough round on the grill grates to parbake. Bake over direct heat for no more than 3 minutes or until it's firm with some grill marks. Flip the pizza with tongs and grill the other side for up to 1 minute. Remove the parbaked dough from the grill and build pizza.

- Spread the sauce evenly over the side that grilled for 3 minutes, leaving a ½ inch along the rim. Layer the cheeses, grilled veggies, and cherry tomatoes. Then place the pizza over direct heat and close the lid. Grill until the cheese is melted, 5–7 minutes. Be sure the lid is closed to capture the convection heat.

- After removing the pizza, slice into wedges and serve warm.

POTATO PIZZA

Adding the right potatoes to a pizza creates a fun texture that surprises people. The key is to thinly slice yellow potatoes using a mandoline (use it safely and at your own risk!). Because they are so thinly sliced, you don't get the starchy taste and they brown slightly in the oven or grill. When layered with a base of crème fraîche and topped with cheese and rosemary, the aroma and the flavor make everyone say, "Wow."

- Preheat your pizza cooker to the target temperature per the instructions on pages 26 through 34.

- On a cookie sheet, lay out the potatoes and lightly salt.

- Form the dough into a round 11–12 inches wide on a floured surface, following the instructions on page 85.

- Move the prepared dough round to a floured pizza peel.

- On your pizza round, spread the crème fraîche to within ½ inch of the rim. Lay out the potatoes, overlapping each other in a circle. Continue until most of the pizza is covered, leaving about ½ inch from the edge. Top with the rosemary and pecorino Romano.

- Transfer the pizza to your cooker and bake per the instructions on pages 26 through 34.

- After removing the pizza, cut into wedges and serve.

YIELD: ONE 12-INCH PIZZA

½ pound yellow potatoes, thinly sliced with a mandoline
¼ teaspoon kosher salt
1 pizza dough
⅓ cup crème fraîche
1 teaspoon chopped fresh rosemary
½ cup grated pecorino Romano

WINE PAIRING: The simplicity of this pizza opens it up to a wide range of flavors, and while rosemary has a strong, distinct taste, it's remarkably friendly with a variety of wines, from white to red. Verdicchio, pinot blanc, or even most sparkling wines are a great match. The crisp acidity of the wines complements the richness of the crème fraîche while the fruity undertones balance out the rosemary and potatoes.

For the salad dressing:

¼ cup extra-virgin olive oil

2 tablespoons freshly
squeezed lemon juice

1 tablespoon Dijon mustard

1 teaspoon honey

¼ teaspoon kosher salt

A turn of freshly cracked
black pepper

For the pizza:

1 pizza dough

2 tablespoons Garlic Oil
(page 105)

⅓ cup shredded low-
moisture mozzarella

⅓ cup grated Asiago

¼ teaspoon red pepper flakes

2 cups mixed greens, dressed
and tossed

WINE PAIRING: This pizza is
topped with a zesty dressing
that adorns the greens.
High-acid salad dressings
want a high-acid wine to
complement. Sauvignon
blanc is a classic choice.
Verdicchio is another fun one
to pair, as are higher-acid
dry-style rieslings.

THE PIZZA SALAD

After testing pizzas for weeks on end for this book, Mary needed
something with greens. A salad (on a pizza) did the trick. Think
of it as cheesy garlic bread meets a fresh, flavorful lightly tossed
salad. It's a great recipe to have on hand at pizza parties for the
parents (read: moms!) trying to sneak some salad into their kids'
diet. Our boys even devour this one! Win-win.

- Preheat your pizza cooker to the target temperature per the instructions
  on pages 26 through 34.

- Combine the oil, lemon juice, mustard, honey, salt, and pepper in a
  medium-size bowl and whisk vigorously to emulsify. Use 2 tablespoons
  of the dressing to toss with the mixed greens. We use the rest of the
  dressing for a mixed green side salad with more greens (or reserve for
  another use).

- Form the dough into a round 11–12 inches wide on a floured surface,
  following the instructions on page 85.

- Move the prepared dough round to a floured pizza peel.

- On your pizza round, brush the garlic oil and layer the cheeses.

- Transfer the pizza to your cooker and bake per the instructions on pages
  26 through 34.

- After removing the pizza, top with the red pepper flakes and dressed
  salad. Cut into wedges and serve. The greens will slightly wilt over the
  hot pizza.

PUT AN EGG ON IT
Breakfast Pizzas That Impress

Weekend mornings just got a whole lot more exciting! Yes, we make pizzas with a breakfast twist. We believe anything you can cook in your kitchen oven or on the stovetop can be cooked outside on your grill or in your smoker (or pizza oven) . . . and it's *so* much better. Even breakfast pizzas.

We guarantee if you have never made a breakfast pizza, it's going to turn heads at your next pizza party. It brings the savory, comforting flavors of brunch to the menu without having to get too technical during the preparation. What really stands out is the addition of eggs. A fresh egg on the pizza will cook in the style of over easy for a delicious flavor profile—and that yolk, when it breaks, adds a lovely richness to any pizza.

A NOTE ON PIZZA OVENS

Pizzas cook quickly in these units, and your jolting of the pizza onto the stone can sometimes cause the egg to break or move around as you slide the pizza into the oven. That's okay.

If the sides of your crust are done before your egg, you can use your smaller turning peel to lift the pizza up, bringing the top of the pizza closer to the heat. Lift it 3–4 inches above the steel base and closer to the flame. This will give the top of the pizza a little broil, finishing it without burning the sides, and it will help your egg finish cooking.

But if you're not feeling the egg, any of these pizzas can be made without it. You can also cook the egg on the side to your desired doneness and style (over easy, fried, etc.), then add it after the pizza is baked. But what's the fun in that?

CHEF'S TIP: When prepping eggs for a breakfast pizza, it's best to crack each one into a small glass dish first. Then slowly pour the egg onto the center of the pizza just before sliding it off your peel and onto the pizza stone. It will cook with the pizza, trust us. If using a grill, you can add the egg onto the pizza after you launch. For smaller pizzas (11–12 inches), we recommend a large egg cracked in the center. If going larger, then two eggs is okay. But you don't want more than one egg on the smaller pies; otherwise, they can get messy and overwhelm the flavor.

THE MORNING SUNSHINE BREAKFAST PIZZA

Inspired by the classic egg breakfast plate, this pizza is covered in crispy bacon, our Garlic Oil, and a cheesy base. The bright flavors of fresh cherry tomatoes offset the richness of the cheese. Top the pizza with a sunny-side egg so the yolk will melt on the pizza when you pull it from the grill or oven.

- Preheat your pizza cooker to the target temperature per the instructions on pages 26 through 34.

- Form the dough into a round 11–12 inches wide on a floured surface, following the instructions on page 85.

- Move the prepared dough round to a floured pizza peel.

- On your pizza round, brush the garlic oil and layer the bacon, tomatoes, and mozzarella. Shake the pizza on the peel to make sure it slides.

- Crack the egg into a small, shallow bowl, taking care not to break the yolk. Carefully place the egg in the center of the pizza.

- Transfer the pizza to your cooker and bake per the instructions on pages 26 through 34.

- After removing the pizza, cut into slices, making sure the yolk breaks in the middle. If the yolk doesn't run, swirl it around the pizza using a butter knife. Serve immediately.

NOTE: To avoid breaking the yolk, nestle the egg in the center with cheese.

YIELD: ONE 12-INCH PIZZA

1 pizza dough
2 tablespoons Garlic Oil (page 105)
3 slices crispy cooked bacon, broken into smaller pieces
¼ cup cherry tomatoes, halved
⅓ cup shredded low-moisture mozzarella
1 large egg

WINE PAIRING: This one calls for a classic mimosa! A little bubbly plus a little orange juice equals happy brunch guests.

YIELD: ONE 12-INCH PIZZA

1 pizza dough
⅓ cup Classic Red Sauce
　(page 107)
½ cup Oaxaca cheese,
　shredded by hand
7 soppressata slices
1 egg

WINE PAIRING: With the sauce, creamy cheese, spicy meat, and rich egg, we've got a few things going on here. Your safest bet is a crisp rosé. Its lively flavors pair well with the salty meat, and crispness balances the richness of the egg. Alternatively, lambrusco's bright, crisp, and fruity notes sing with this dish.

SOPPRESSATA AND EGG PIZZA

Soppressata is a dry-cured pork salami that can be sweet or spicy. It can taste slightly different depending on where you purchase it, but it will usually melt in your mouth with richness. Think of it as pepperoni's more sophisticated, elegant sibling. Combined with the egg and cheese, this is a rich and luxurious breakfast treat.

- Preheat your pizza cooker to the target temperature per the instructions on pages 26 through 34.

- Form the dough into a round 11–12 inches wide on a floured surface, following the instructions on page 85.

- Move the prepared dough round to a floured pizza peel.

- On your pizza round, spread the sauce to within a ½ inch of the rim. Layer with even-sized strips of the cheese and the soppressata.

- Crack the egg into a small, shallow bowl, taking care not to break the yolk. Carefully place the egg in the center of the pizza.

- Transfer the pizza to your cooker and bake per the instructions on pages 26 through 34.

- After removing the pizza, cut into slices, making sure the yolk breaks in the middle. If the yolk doesn't run, swirl it around the pizza using a butter knife. Serve immediately.

THE BISCUITS AND GRAVY PIZZA

A good biscuits and gravy breakfast is one of Sean's weaknesses. We had to figure out a way to combine these delicious flavors to craft the breakfast pizza of his dreams. Treating the dough like the "biscuits" creates the perfect base before layering on the creamy, flavorful sausage gravy. Oh my goodness. We don't know if we will be able to go back to the traditional version after this heavenly pizza. This one works with or without an egg. Dealer's choice!

- Preheat your pizza cooker to the target temperature per the instructions on pages 26 through 34.

- Form the dough into a round 11–12 inches wide on a floured surface, following the instructions on page 85.

- Move the prepared dough round to a floured pizza peel.

- On your pizza round, spread the white sauce within ½ inch of the rim. Layer the sausage and cheese, then sprinkle with sage.

- Crack the egg into a shallow bowl and gently add to the center of the pizza.

- Transfer the pizza to your cooker and bake per the instructions on pages 26 through 34.

- After removing the pizza, set on a cutting board and dust with the black pepper and a sprinkle of paprika. Cut into wedges, so the yolk breaks in the middle. Serve warm.

CHEF'S TIP: If you want an even sprinkle of paprika, add 1 teaspoon to a fine strainer. Tap the strainer while hovering over the pizza, using the palm of your hand or a heavy knife. This will dust the pizza as evenly as gently falling snow.

YIELD: ONE 12-INCH PIZZA

1 pizza dough
¼ cup Basic White Sauce (page 108)
½ cup cooked bulk breakfast sausage or hot Italian sausage, crumbled
2 ounces fresh mozzarella, broken up by hand into chunks
¼ cup chopped fresh sage
1 egg
Freshly cracked black pepper, for sprinkling
Smoked paprika, for sprinkling

WINE PAIRING: The acidity in a crisp chenin blanc is nice to cut through the rich and flavorful gravy and brightens up this hearty dish. A fruity rosé also does the trick; if you want a red, reach for a barbera or acidic Italian wine to complement that spicy sausage.

YIELD: ONE 12-INCH PIZZA

For the hollandaise:

¼ cup unsalted butter

2 egg yolks

1 tablespoon freshly squeezed lemon juice

¼ teaspoon kosher salt

¼ teaspoon smoked paprika

For the pizza:

1 pizza dough

2 tablespoons Garlic Oil (page 105)

½ cup shredded low-moisture mozzarella

½ cup diced cooked asparagus (about 8 spears)

3 ounces Canadian bacon, sliced with each round cut in half

2 eggs

¼ cup diced chives

1 turn of freshly cracked black pepper

WINE PAIRING: Nothing says brunch better than bubbly, and nothing pairs with a rich hollandaise sauce or a poached egg better than sparkling wine. Go with a crisp cava or brut sparkling to cut through the sauce and refresh your palate.

BENEDICT PIZZA

Nothing defines brunch better than a classic eggs Benedict. Move over English muffin, there's a new carb in town that's perfect as a base for a poached egg, salty slice of meat, and heavenly hollandaise sauce. While not an ingredient in a traditional Benedict, asparagus is a beloved complement to the hollandaise. Just make sure to precook the asparagus. It's easiest to roast it in the oven for 12 minutes at 425 degrees F.

- To make the hollandaise: In a small saucepan over medium heat, melt the butter.

- In a medium-size bowl, add the egg yolks, lemon juice, salt, and paprika. Whisk to combine and break the yolks. Slowly add the melted butter in small increments while you are whisking the egg yolk mixture. Continue to whisk and add butter until it's all combined, emulsified, and thickened.

- Preheat your pizza cooker to the target temperature per the instructions on pages 26 through 34.

- Form the dough into a round 11–12 inches wide on a floured surface, following the instructions on page 85.

- Move the prepared dough round to a floured pizza peel.

- On your pizza round, spread the garlic oil. Layer the cheese, asparagus, and Canadian bacon halves.

- Crack the eggs into a shallow bowl and carefully add to opposite areas of the pizza.

- Transfer the pizza to your cooker and bake per the instructions on pages 26 through 34.

- After removing the pizza, set on a cutting board and drizzle with the hollandaise sauce, chives, and black pepper. Cut into slices and serve warm.

NOTE: If you make your hollandaise too early, it can cool and thicken. If that happens, then add 1 teaspoon of hot water and whisk. Continue to add a teaspoon of hot water until the sauce reaches your desired consistency.

HUEVOS RANCHEROS PIZZA

The ultimate cure for a hangover, or just a hungry stomach. Classic huevos rancheros have a rich and runny sauce, but we found that it made the pizza too watery. Instead, we're topping the finished pizza with a fresh salsa to avoid adding too much liquid to the pizza.

The classic version of this breakfast also includes a fried egg. If you want to go that route, we are totally on your team. Just fry the eggs on the side, and top the finished pizza with the fried eggs as soon as the pizza comes off the grill or out of the oven. Garnish everything with more salsa.

- To make the refried beans mix, in a small saucepan over medium heat, combine the refried beans, water, and pico de gallo. Stir to combine and bring to a simmer. Continue stirring for 4 minutes. Add more water as needed to get a soft texture that easily comes off a spoon for spreading on your pizza.

- Preheat your pizza cooker to the target temperature per the instructions on pages 26 through 34.

- Form the dough into a round 11–12 inches wide on a floured surface, following the instructions on page 85.

- Move the prepared dough round to a floured pizza peel.

- On your pizza round, layer the refried beans mix, cheese, jalapeños, and green chile. Shake the pizza on the peel to make sure it slides.

- Crack the egg into a small, shallow bowl, taking care not to break the yolk. Carefully place the egg in the center of the pizza.

- Transfer the pizza to your cooker and bake per the instructions on pages 26 through 34.

- After removing the pizza, top with pico de gallo and cut into slices, making sure the yolk breaks in the middle. If the yolk doesn't run, swirl it with a butter knife around the pizza. Serve immediately.

YIELD: ONE 12-INCH PIZZA

For the refried beans mix (enough for two pizzas):
1 (15-ounce) can refried beans
¼ cup water
¼ cup pico de gallo or salsa, store-bought or find our recipes at Vindulge.com

For the pizza:
1 pizza dough
½ cup refried beans mix (see above)
½ cup Oaxaca cheese, shredded by hand
¼ cup thinly sliced jalapeños
2 tablespoons roasted and diced green chile
1 egg
¼ cup pico de gallo

WINE PAIRING: It may feel risqué to drink red wine with breakfast, but it works here. We love an earthy carménère with this dish, but it pairs equally well with something a little lighter, such as a gamay noir or pinot noir.

SUGAR RUSH

Dessert Pizzas

When we introduce people to dessert-style pizzas, most are skeptical. But when you balance sweetness with other ingredients, the flavor profiles are off the charts. It also becomes an instant conversation with any guests who have never had a sweeter-style pizza.

RED WINE POACHED PEAR PIZZA

Poaching pears in red wine prior to making the pizza infuses them with a deliciously rich flavor reminiscent of mulled wine. It adds a depth of flavor to the pizza that would otherwise be bland. It's definitely worth the extra step. Be careful not to use overripe pears because they will be too soft and fall apart. We love to top the pizza with some candied walnuts or pecans after it's been baked for added texture and a touch of sweetness. And don't be shy with the honey. If you don't have hot honey, you can use regular honey. Depending on how large your pears are, you may not need two. But better to start with two just in case!

- To make the poached pears, place wine, orange juice, orange peel, sugar, and cinnamon stick in a medium-size stockpot and bring to a boil. Add pears, then reduce to a simmer and cover. Note that the pears won't be completely submerged.

- Simmer for 20 minutes, rotating the pears every 5 minutes for even poaching.

- Remove with a slotted spoon when they are just starting to become soft (but not too soft). Immediately transfer to an ice bath for 1 minute.

- Place pears on a drying rack lined with paper towels to remove excess moisture.

- To make the pizza, preheat your pizza cooker to the target temperature per instructions on pages 26 through 34.

- Slice the pears into thin slices and cut around any core or seeds.

- Form the dough into a round 11–12 inches wide on a floured surface, following the instructions on page 85.

$\longrightarrow$

YIELD: ONE 12-INCH PIZZA ROUND

For the poached pears:
4 pears, slightly underripe, and skin removed
2 cups bold red wine (such as a cabernet sauvignon or petite sirah)
½ cup freshly squeezed orange juice (from about 1 large orange)
1 (3-inch) orange peel (we recommend peeling before juicing)
¼ cup cane sugar
1 (3-inch) cinnamon stick

For the pizza:
1 pizza dough
2 poached pears, cored and thinly sliced
2 ounces ricotta, broken up into smaller pieces by hand
2 tablespoons crushed candied walnuts or pecans
A drizzle of Classic Hot Honey (about 1 tablespoon, page 112)
¼ teaspoon finishing salt

WINE PAIRING: We've entered dessert territory here, but don't be scared. This is a mildly flavored dessert pizza with the cooked pears and touch of hot honey leading the way. Passito di Pantelleria is a very special dessert wine from the island of Pantelleria, just off Sicily, made from sun-dried grapes, resulting in a sweet wine with deep flavor and great acidity. It's like a dream with this pizza. Otherwise, look for a sweeter-style sparkling or semisweet riesling to pair with this decadent dessert.

- Move the prepared dough round to a floured pizza peel. Evenly layer the poached pears facing the same direction around the pizza (don't stack). Using a spoon, drop ricotta evenly around the pizza.

- Transfer pizza to your cooker and bake per instructions on pages 26 through 34. After removing from the pizza oven, drizzle with hot honey and top with the chopped candied nuts. Cut into wedges and serve.

SPICED APPLE AND SALTED CARAMEL PIZZA

Take the warm flavors and aromas reminiscent of apple pie and add some salted caramel for a dessert pizza that everyone will talk about. Start with a sweet, cinnamon-sugar butter base and some apples tossed in lemon and apple pie spices. Then finish with a homemade caramel sauce. A pizza for apple pie lovers!

- Preheat your pizza cooker to the target temperature per instructions on pages 26 through 34.

- In a small bowl, combine the butter, sugar, and cinnamon. In a large bowl toss the apple slices, lemon juice, and apple pie spice.

- Form your dough into a round 11–12 inches wide on a floured surface, following the instructions on page 85.

- Move the prepared dough round to a floured pizza peel. Coat the dough base with the cinnamon-sugar butter. Layer the apples facing the same direction around the pizza in one layer.

- Transfer pizza to your cooker and bake per instructions on pages 26 through 34. After removing from the pizza oven, drizzle with caramel sauce. Cut into wedges and serve.

$\longrightarrow$

YIELD: ONE 12-INCH PIZZA

1 pizza dough
2 tablespoons softened unsalted butter
½ tablespoon cane sugar
1 teaspoon ground cinnamon
2 small crisp red apples (such as Fuji), cored and thinly sliced
½ lemon, juiced
1 teaspoon apple pie spice
2 tablespoons salted caramel sauce (recipe follows)

WINE PAIRING: The apple pie portion of this pizza isn't overly sweet. But adding that decadent caramel sauce gives the pie a kiss of sugary sweetness. If you want to go big try a Sauternes, a sweet full-bodied wine named after the French region where it's produced. Ice wine, particularly made from riesling grapes, would be my second choice. You could also go with a sweet style of Champagne, like a demi-sec or doux (terms indicating its level of sweetness).

Salted Caramel Sauce

YIELD: 1 ¼ CUP

1 cup cane sugar
6 tablespoons room-temperature
  unsalted butter, cut into cubes
½ cup heavy cream

½ teaspoon kosher salt (If you want
  saltier flavor then you can bump
  up to 1 teaspoon)

- In a medium size, stainless-steel saucepan over medium-low heat add cane sugar. Stir continuously with a wooden spoon. The sugar will start to melt and get clumpy which is normal. Keep stirring until the sugar has liquefied. Reduce heat if you smell any burning or see scorching around the sides of the pan.

- Once the sugar has melted add the butter and continue to stir. The butter will melt rapidly, and you'll see some bubbling. Keep stirring over the medium-low heat until the butter has completely melted.

- Add the heavy cream and continue to stir. As the cream is added, expect the caramel sauce to bubble significantly. Keep stirring continuously and let it simmer for up to 1 minute.

- Remove from heat and add the salt. Continue to stir for another few seconds. Expect some bubbling to occur for up to 1 minute. Let cool before serving. Caramel sauce can be stored in the refrigerator for up to 6 months.

- To reheat the sauce, microwave in 30-second intervals until softened. Alternatively, you can use a double boiler. Add water to a saucepan and bring to a boil over high heat. In a stainless steel bowl, add the sauce. Reduce the boiling water to a simmer and place the bowl with sauce over the pan. Stir until it softens.

S'MORES PIZZA

A twist on a childhood classic, the secret to this campfire-inspired pizza is to parbake the dough. This allows it to cook along with the cinnamon-sugar butter; otherwise, the chocolate will scorch and taste bitter. Then, once the crust is just about done, pull it out, top it with the chocolate chips, crushed graham crackers, and marshmallows, and place it back in the pizza oven or grill to finish. You'll know it's done the same way you know your s'mores are done—the marshmallows will be toasted and the chocolate melted (but not burnt). It only takes a few seconds, so stay close. Get ready for a pizza that transports you straight back to the days of sticky fingers and campfire stories.

- Preheat your pizza cooker to the target temperature per the instructions on pages 26 through 34.

- In a small bowl, combine the butter, sugar, and cinnamon.

- Form the dough into a round 11–12 inches wide on a floured surface, following the instructions on page 85.

- Move the prepared dough round to a floured pizza peel.

- On your pizza round, spread the cinnamon butter with the back of a spoon to within ½ inch of the rim.

- Transfer the pizza to your cooker, and parbake until the dough is *almost* done and the cinnamon butter is bubbling.

- After removing the pizza, add the chocolate chips, graham crackers, and marshmallows.

- Return your pizza to the cooker, then remove when the chips have melted and the marshmallows have browned. It will happen quickly.

- Slice into squares and serve.

NOTE: If using a pizza oven, be sure you turn the pizza every few seconds. The flame will be hot, so the marshmallows can burn or catch fire just like a campfire s'more when you get too close to the flames. It will cook slower on a grill at a lower heat, as the pizza is further from the heat source.

YIELD: ONE 12-INCH PIZZA

¼ cup softened unsalted butter
1 teaspoon cane sugar
½ teaspoon ground cinnamon
1 pizza dough
⅓ cup milk chocolate chips
2 graham crackers, crushed
1 cup mini marshmallows

WINE PAIRING: This recipe may recall a childhood favorite, but it requires an adult pairing. We love a ruby port wine with this pizza. This younger-style fortified wine has a sweet, rich, and deeply fruity flavor and is one of a very few great matches for melted milk chocolate and marshmallows.

THE OREGON BERRY PIZZA

Oregon blackberries and raspberries make up over 95 percent of the frozen berries sold in the United States, so it's only natural to celebrate them with our berry pie. You can make this pizza with fresh berries that are in season or with frozen berries year-round. There are so many fun, fresh, and lightly sweet flavors dancing on your slice in this colorful creation!

- Preheat your pizza cooker to the target temperature per the instructions on pages 27 through 34.

- In a small bowl, combine the berries, sugar, cinnamon, and 1 teaspoon of the lemon juice. Stir to combine and let macerate. This can be done the day before.

- In another small bowl, combine the mascarpone, remaining teaspoon of lemon juice, and lemon zest.

- Form the dough into a round 11–12 inches wide on a floured surface, following the instructions on page 85.

- Move the prepared dough round to a floured pizza peel.

- On your pizza round, spread out the butter with the back of a spoon to within ½ inch of the rim. Layer on the mascarpone mixture and then top with the berries.

- Transfer the pizza to your cooker and bake per the instructions on pages 26 through 34.

- After removing the pizza, drizzle with the hot honey and sprinkle with basil. Cut into wedges and serve.

NOTE: If using frozen berries, follow the package directions for thawing and strain.

YIELD: ONE 12-INCH PIZZA

½ cup blackberries, rinsed and dried

½ cup raspberries, rinsed and dried

½ teaspoon cane sugar

1 teaspoon ground cinnamon

2 teaspoons lemon juice, divided

¼ cup mascarpone

1 teaspoon lemon zest

1 pizza dough

2 tablespoons softened unsalted butter

1 teaspoon Classic Hot Honey (page 112)

¼ cup thinly sliced fresh basil

WINE PAIRING: Steer clear of dry wines for this pizza. You want something a little on the sweet side to harmonize with those sugar-laden berries. Late-harvest riesling is beautiful with this, as is a bubbly Moscato d'Asti. The wine's sweet, fruity notes and mild effervescence cut through the creamy mascarpone and stand up to the fruity nature of the pizza.

YIELD: ONE 12-INCH PIZZA

For the icing:

2 tablespoons softened
    unsalted butter

1 cup powdered sugar

2 tablespoons whole milk

1 teaspoon vanilla extract

For the crumble:

¼ cup room-temperature
    unsalted butter

¼ cup all-purpose flour

¼ cup brown sugar
    (dark or light)

2 teaspoons ground
    cinnamon

1 pizza dough
    (we recommend
    the All-Purpose New
    York–Inspired Dough,
    page 100)

WINE PAIRING: If we're
being honest, we feel like
this is a better match for
hot chocolate or a cup of
sweetened coffee. But if
we're going there, we're
drinking it with a ruby port.
The fruitiness and richness
of the fortified wine is one
of the few things that can
stand up to the sweet,
creamy icing and sugar fest
of a pizza. Cheers!

CINNAMON ROLL PIZZA

Cinnamon rolls are our traditional Christmas morning breakfast.
It involves quite the process to make good ones. This version
is done in a fraction of the time and has all those nostalgic and
sweet, festive flavors, with none of the complicated steps. It took
a few tries to find a version the kids loved as much as our holiday
morning classic, and this is it.

We recommend cooking this with a pizza stone at 500 degrees
F (and in an oven at no more than 600 degrees) to avoid scorching
the topping. Let it cook at a lower temperature and you'll thank us
for the results.

- Preheat your cooker to no more than 600 degrees F (with a pizza stone
  at 500 degrees F).

- To make the icing, combine the butter with the powdered sugar, milk,
  and vanilla extract and whisk until your desired texture. If too thick, add
  1 teaspoon of milk at a time until it's thin enough to drizzle over the
  pizza. Set aside.

- For the crumble, combine the butter, flour, sugar, and cinnamon. It will
  be slightly thick and dry.

- Form the dough into a round 11–12 inches wide on a floured surface,
  following the instructions on page 85.

- Move the prepared dough round to a floured pizza peel.

- On your pizza round, spread the crumble in small chunks to within
  ½ inch of the rim.

- Transfer the pizza to your cooker and bake until the dough is cooked
  through and the sugar is caramelized.

- After removing the pizza, drizzle with the icing. Cut into slices and serve.

PIZZA PARTY

Pizza brings people together. Think about it. At the end of any kids' sports season, where do the teams go to celebrate? A pizza place. What food do you have delivered when the kids have a sleepover or birthday party with friends? Pizza. What meal is synonymous with Friday nights? Pizza, at least at our house. What is a meal almost all can agree on? Pizza.

And pizza parties are the best when they are interactive. We will tell you from experience that if you're inviting twenty people over for a pizza night, you don't want to be the one slinging pizzas *all night*; otherwise, you won't get to talk to any of your guests. So when someone asks to help, say yes.

This is why it's fun to teach your guests how to make a pizza, then hand the tools over to them to let them craft their own pie. It's interactive for everyone and you get to be as social as you want with your guests.

The pizzas may not all come out as perfect as from a restaurant when you put your friends in charge. But that's okay. They will have fun making their own pizzas and be proud of the way they look (even if the shape turns out more like the state of Florida than a round pie).

Here's a handy checklist for planning and hosting a pizza party.

MENU PLANNING

- Pick three pizza recipes. You'll usually have extra cheese and toppings to improvise more.
- Plan for one pizza for each person. Trust us.
- One large appetizer for every ten people. This is a great dish to delegate to a guest.
- One bottle of wine for every two adults.
- For every five people, plan a salad or side. These are other good candidates for delegating to a guest.

THE DAY PRIOR

- Go shopping.
- Prepare the dough.
- Make the sauces.
- Slice and prep all the ingredients.
- Chill the wine.

THE DAY OF

- Set up the biggest cutting board you have.
- Lay out all your ingredients in bowls and trays.
- Set aside a bowl with extra semolina flour.
- Have your pizza oven or grill at temperature as people arrive.

ACKNOWLEDGMENTS

What a wild and delicious journey this book has been! We are ridiculously grateful to so many amazing souls who helped make this book happen.

First and foremost to the amazing community of friends and neighbors that we are lucky to be surrounded by out here in wine country. You are the greatest taste testers, feedback providers, and wild idea creators. We love our pizza and wine parties with you all and hope to keep this tradition for years to come! (Even the ones that don't end until 3:00 a.m.!)

To Cole and Sawyer, our most honest taste testers of all. You two are everything and our reason for doing all of this. Thank you for putting up with a diet of nearly nonstop pizza for so many months.

To so many amazing trailblazers of pizza who have come before us and inspired our work, including Ken Forkish and Tony Gemignani whose books are essential on our bookshelf.

To Yolanda Cressler for always being willing to fly out here to watch the boys (even in the cold, wet winter months), clean up our pizza messes, take care of our crazy chickens, run errands, and make meals, you are always here for whatever we need help with! We love you! And to Patricia Martin for always providing meaningful moral support and confidence building.

To Adam Ruplinger for your honest feedback and brilliant ideas, and for helping to make the pizzas seen in the photos of this book so darn beautiful and easy to photograph. To Justin Myers for taking Mary under your wings and providing photography mentorship, as well as some awesome photos for this book! You gave Mary the confidence to shoot this book. And to Sarah Schoenbine and Kristin Bennett for your great styling talents and for helping to bring the photos in this book alive. Mary couldn't have taken such pretty pictures without your help!

To our incredible and supportive team at Sasquatch: Jennifer Worick, Tony Ong, and Isabella Hardie. You are such a wonderful and understanding group to work with. Thank you for turning our ideas into such a beautiful and fun book and continuing to trust that we can produce cookbooks that help people thrive and create great backyard experiences. And to Martha Hopkins, our agent who took a chance on this random couple from Oregon who like to cook things over fire and drink wine (not always in that order).

Last, but certainly not least, our amazing Vindulge community and readers! You are our reason for creating and we appreciate each and every one of you. Your support day after day is why we can create all of our content. In the end, we do it for you!

RESOURCES

Grills We Use and Recommend
Kamado: XLarge Big Green Egg
Big Green Egg Pizza Oven Wedge
biggreenegg.com

Kettle: Original Kettle Premium Charcoal
Grill 22-inch
weber.com

Pellet Grills
Yoder Smokers: Great luxury pellet grill with
pizza accessory.
yodersmokers.com

Camp Chef
campchef.com

Gas Grills
Weber Genesis
weber.com

Pizza Ovens That Are Awesome
Portable and All Purpose: Solo Stove Pi
solostove.com

Baking and Pizza: Gozney Dome
gozney.com

Best Capacity and Luxury Oven: Alfa Forni
alfaforni.com

Great Fuel
Big Green Egg Hardwood Lump Charcoal
biggreenegg.com

Jealous Devil lump charcoal
jealousdevil.com

Pizza Wood
Cutting Edge Firewood: Multiple size options
and includes starters and matches.
cuttingedgefirewood.com

Tumbleweed Fire Starters
Cutting Edge Firewood tumbleweed fire
starters
cuttingedgefirewood.com

Thermometers
Thermoworks Thermapen One instant-read
thermometer
Thermoworks Hi-Temp Industrial IR
thermometer
thermoworks.com

Knives and Pizza Cutters
Dalstrong
dalstrong.com

INDEX

This book is dedicated to our amazing community of friends and neighbors, who have always celebrated community through food, wine, and gatherings. Here's to the many pizza parties to come. Cheers!

Printed in China

SASQUATCH BOOKS with colophon is a registered trademark of Blue Star Press, LLC

29 28 27 26 25   9 8 7 6 5 4 3 2 1

Editors: Jen Worick and Jill Saginario
Production editor: Isabella Hardie
Designer: Tony Ong

Photos on pages viii, iv, 3, 9, 10, 12, 15, 37, 40, 77, 84, 202–203
© Justin Myers

Library of Congress Cataloging-in-Publication Data is available.

The recipes contained in this book have been created for the ingredients and techniques indicated. Neither publisher nor author is responsible for your specific health or allergy needs that may require supervision. Nor are publisher and author responsible for any adverse reactions you may have to the recipes contained in the book, whether you follow them as written or modify them to suit your personal dietary needs or tastes.

ISBN: 978-1-63217-541-0

Sasquatch Books
1325 Fourth Avenue, Suite 1025
Seattle, WA 98101

SasquatchBooks.com